ROBIN'S GUIDE TO BEING COOL(ER)

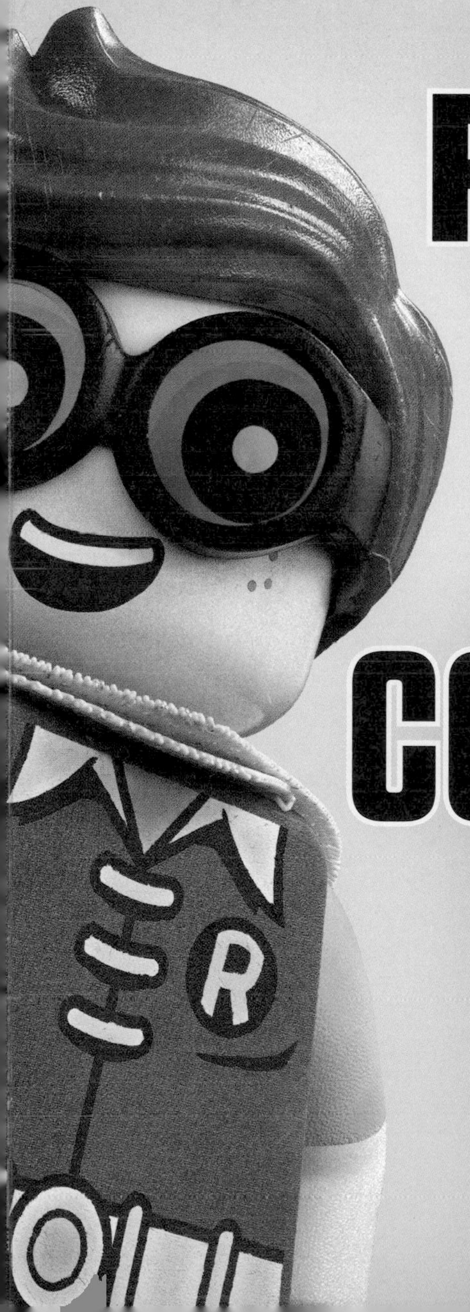
R

BY MEREDITH RUSU

SCHOLASTIC INC.

Published by Scholastic Inc., *Publishers since 1920*. SCHOLASTIC
and associated logos are trademarks and/or registered
trademarks of Scholastic Inc.

The publisher does not have any control over and does not assume any
responsibility for author or third-party websites or their content.

This book is a work of fiction. Names, characters, places, and incidents
are either the product of the author's imagination or are used fictitiously,
and any resemblance to actual persons, living or dead, business
establishments, events, or locales is entirely coincidental.

ISBN 978-1-338-21840-4

10 9 8 7 6 5 4 3 2 1   17 18 19 20 21
Printed in the U.S.A.   40

First printing 2017
Book design by Jessica Meltzer and Theresa Venezia

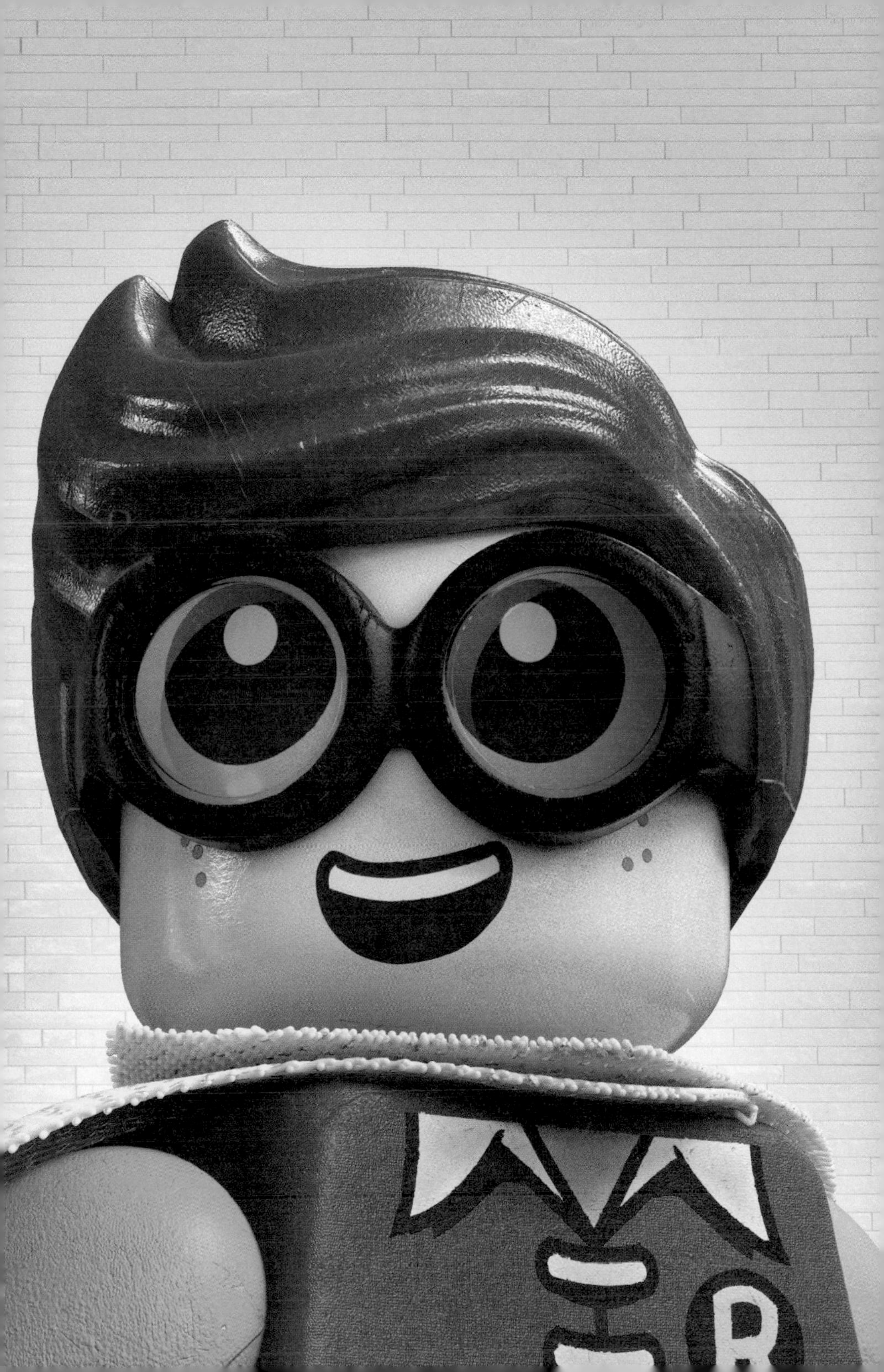

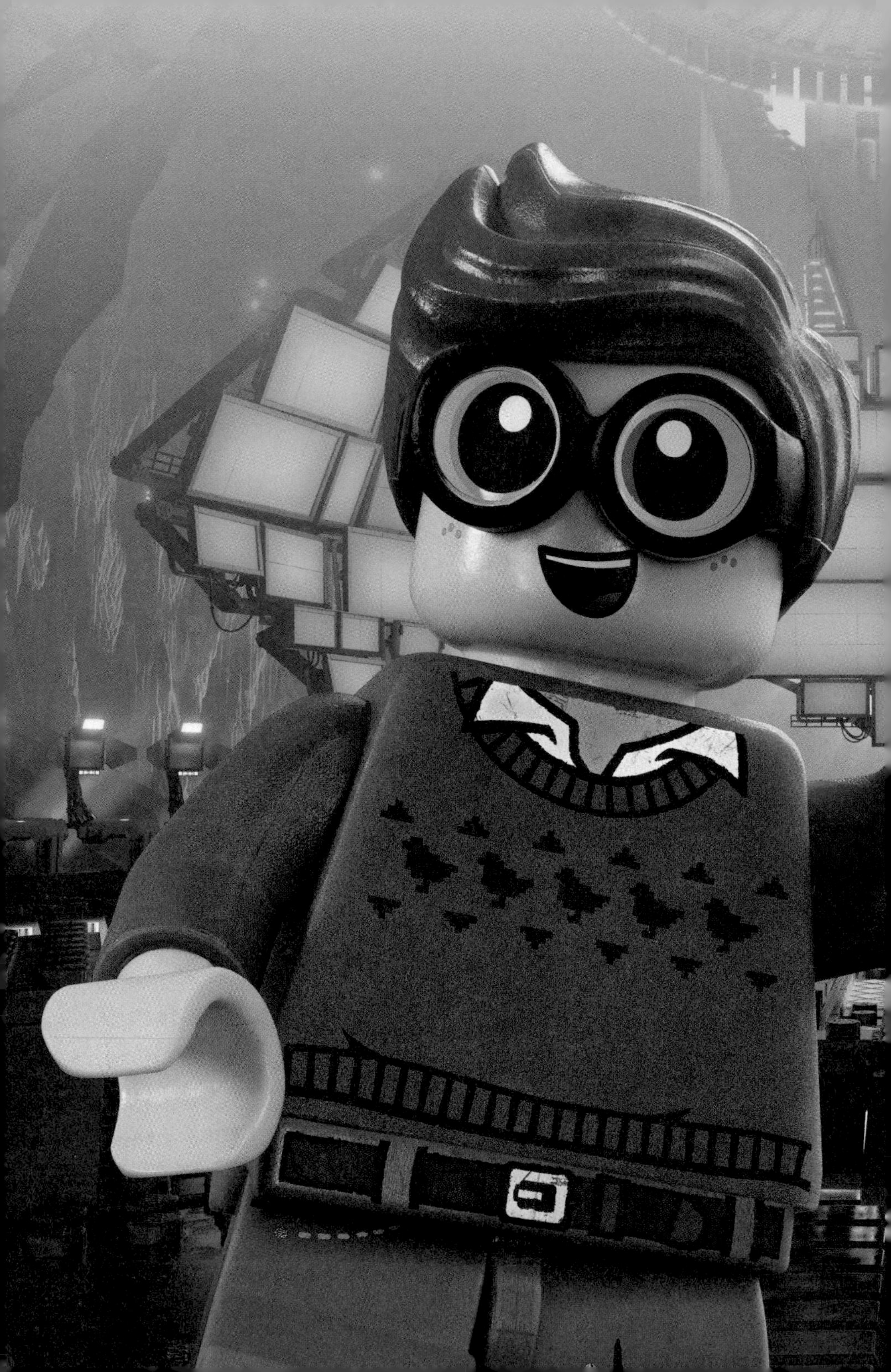

CONTENTS

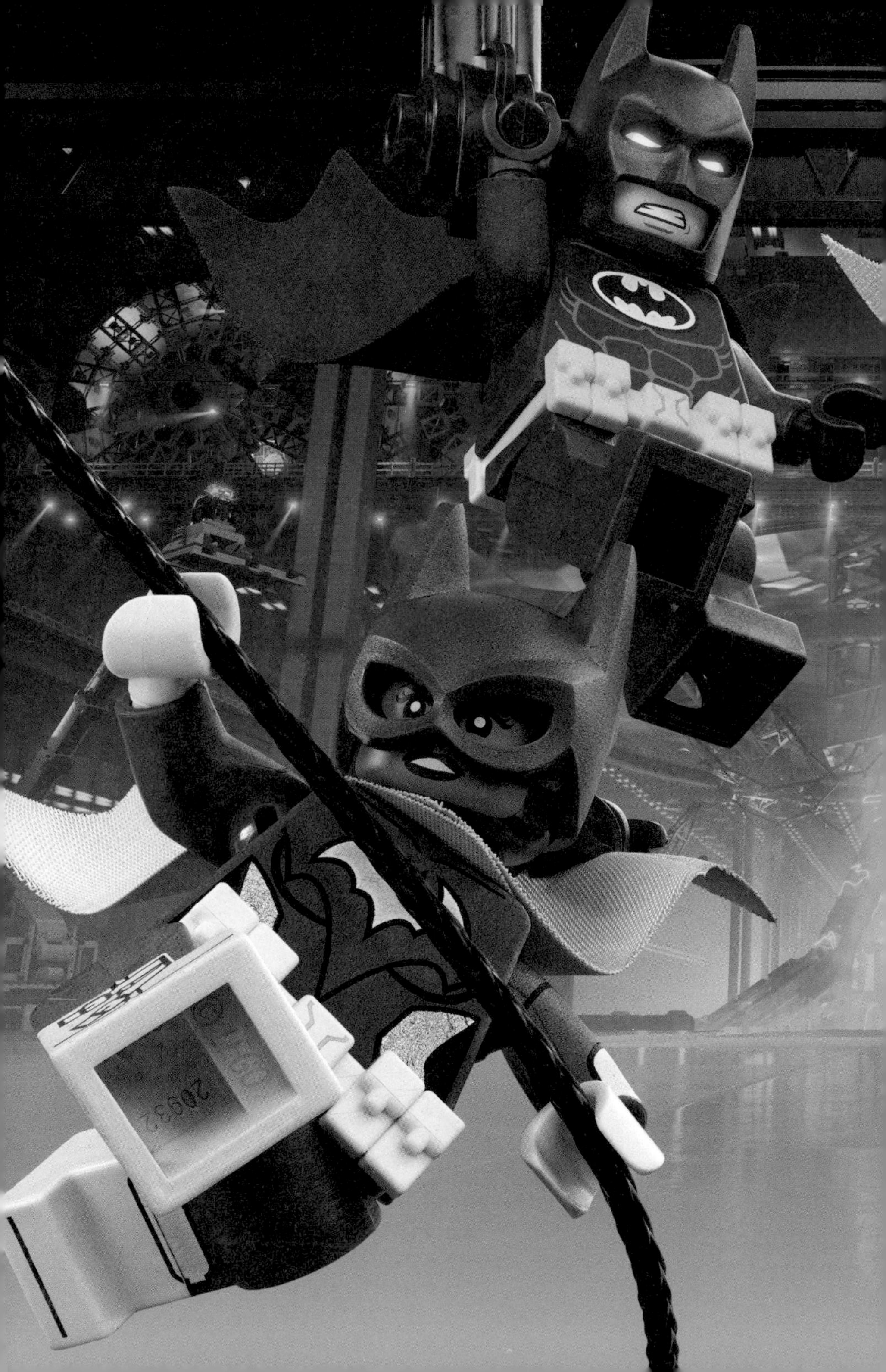

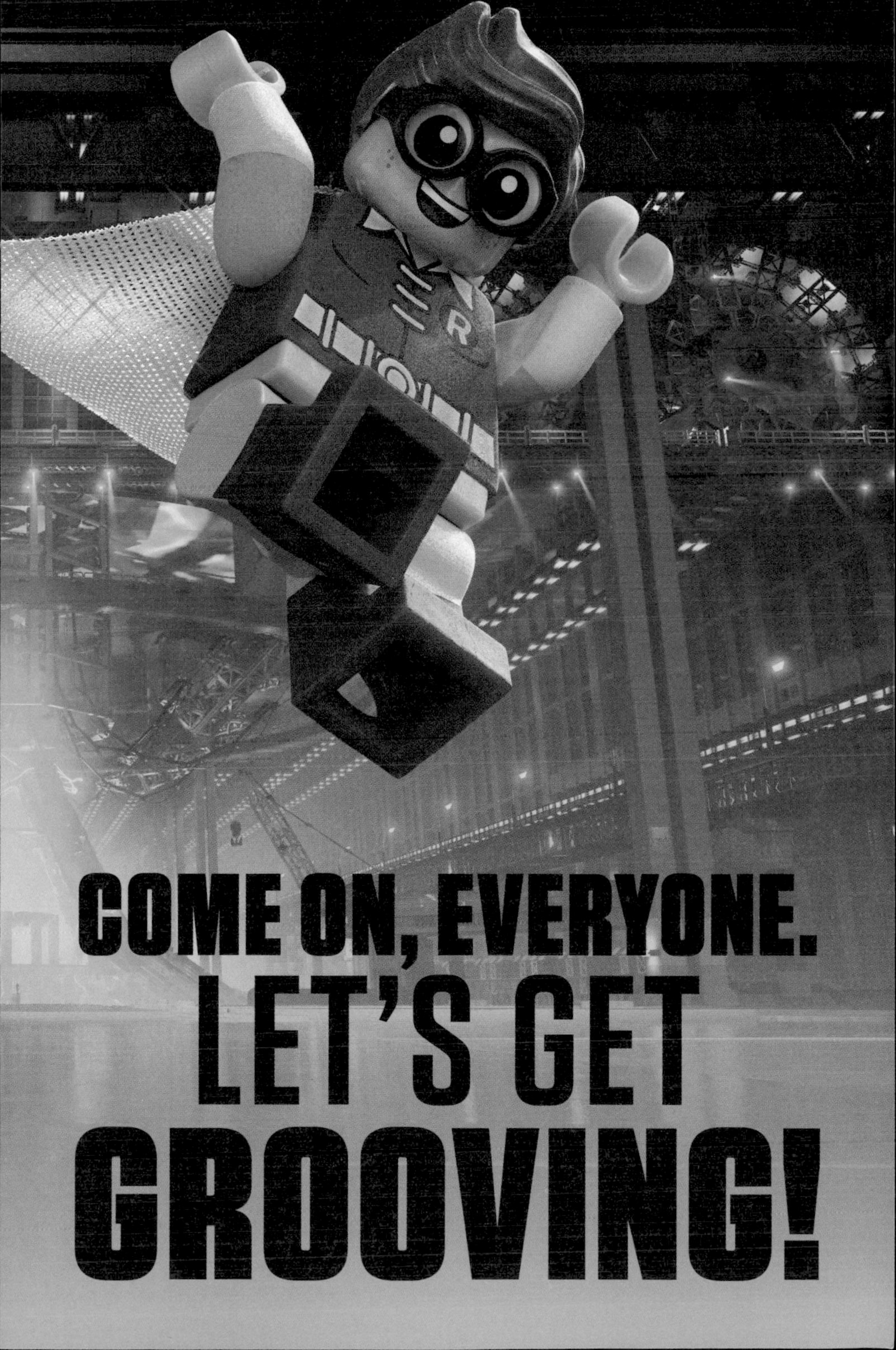

COME ON, EVERYONE.
LET'S GET
GROOVING!

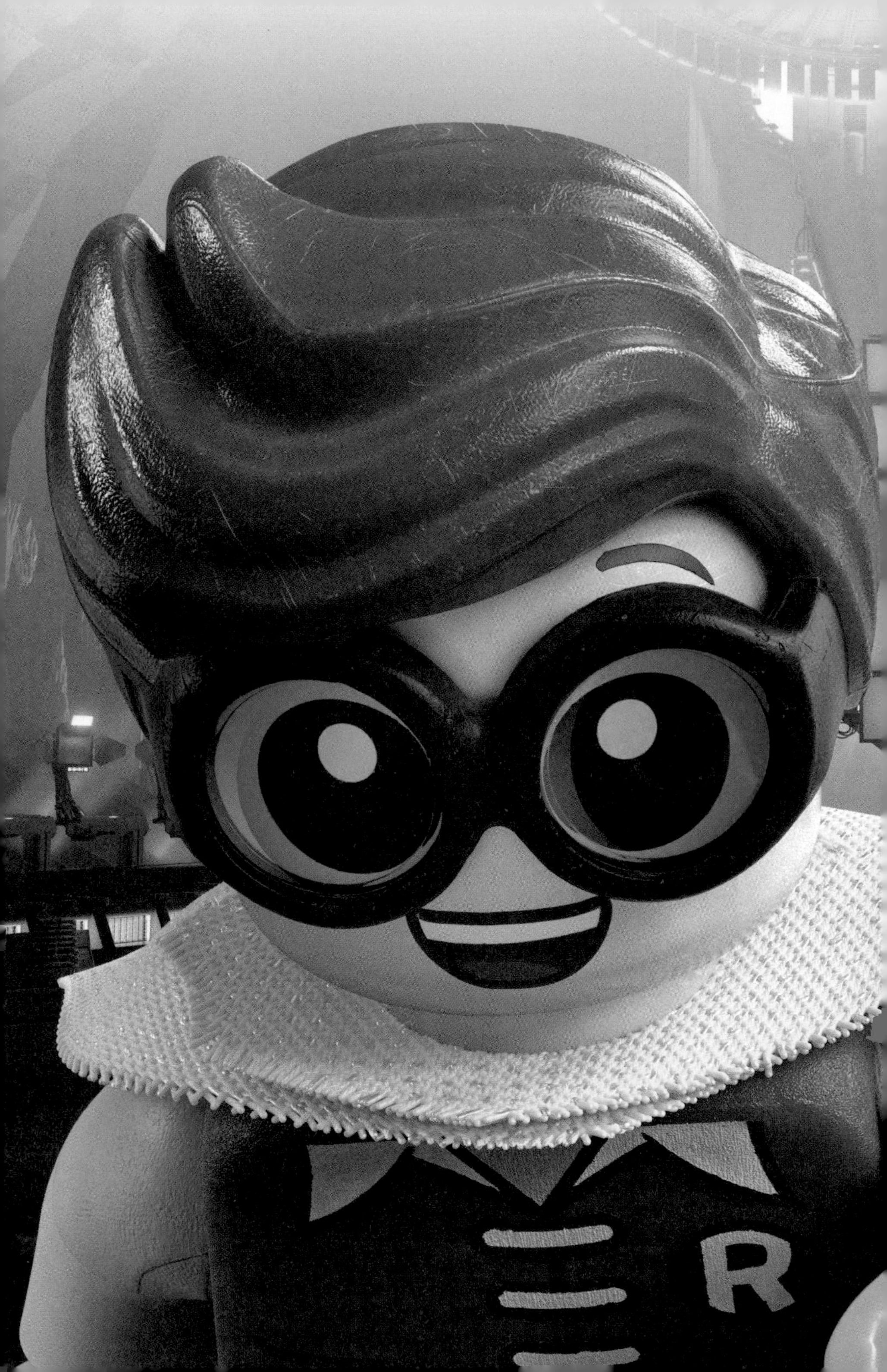
R

INTRODUCTION

OH MY G-O-S-H, HI! I'm Robin, and boy, I'm just so jazzed you're reading this book. That's because I've got something important to tell you.

You know about Batman, right? I mean, of course you do. Who doesn't know about Batman? He's the best! He's also my dad. One of two dads, actually. And then they turned out to be the same dad . . . well, it's a long story.

But here's the important thing. Since I've been hanging out so much with Batman (my dad), and going on super-secret missions with my old man, and enjoying quality one-on-one time with my pops, I've learned all his tips for being cool. And I'm going to teach you everything I've learned! You'll be the coolest of the cool!

Well, only Batman is *the* coolest. So, let's just say you'll be cool(er). In fact, by the time you're done reading this book, you'll be cooler than ever. Groovy!

MY NEW FAMILY

I wasn't always cool(er). My code name may be Robin, but my real name is Dick Grayson. I used to be a lonely little orphan at Gotham City Orphanage. Then I got adopted by Daddy-o #1, billionaire Bruce Wayne. That's when my life changed forever.

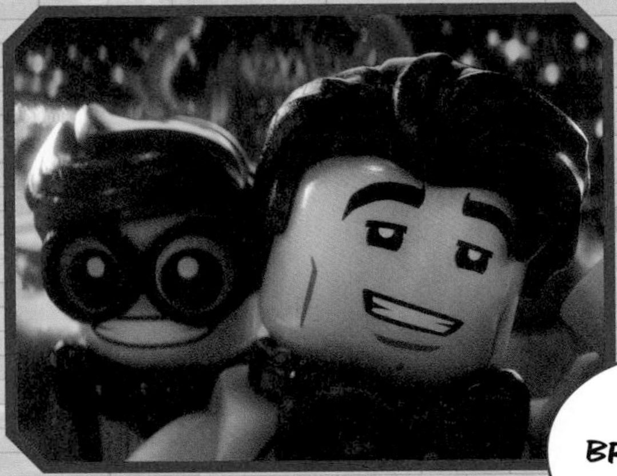

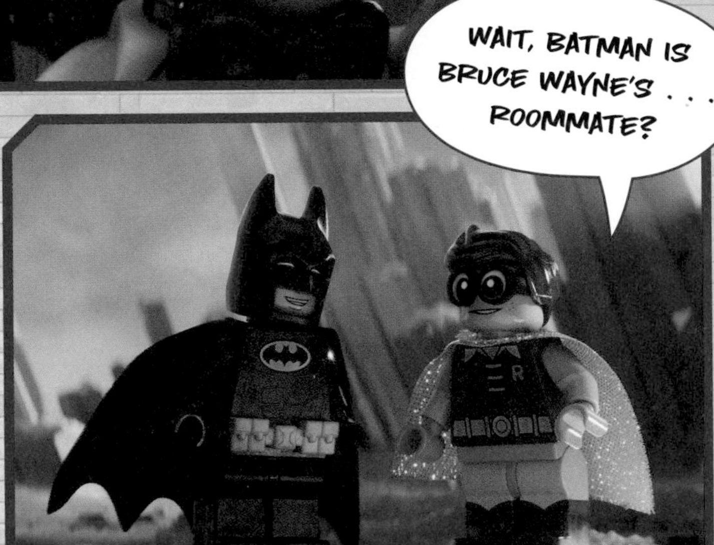
WAIT, BATMAN IS BRUCE WAYNE'S . . . ROOMMATE?

ME AND MY DAD(S)

I met Mr. Wayne at a fancy party where my orphan choir was performing. He said he was interested in adopting a son—yay! And that son turned out to be ME! Woo-hoo!

Little did I know, Bruce Wayne is . . . *shhhhhhh*, this is a big secret . . . Batman! That means I have TWO dads, and one of them is Batman!

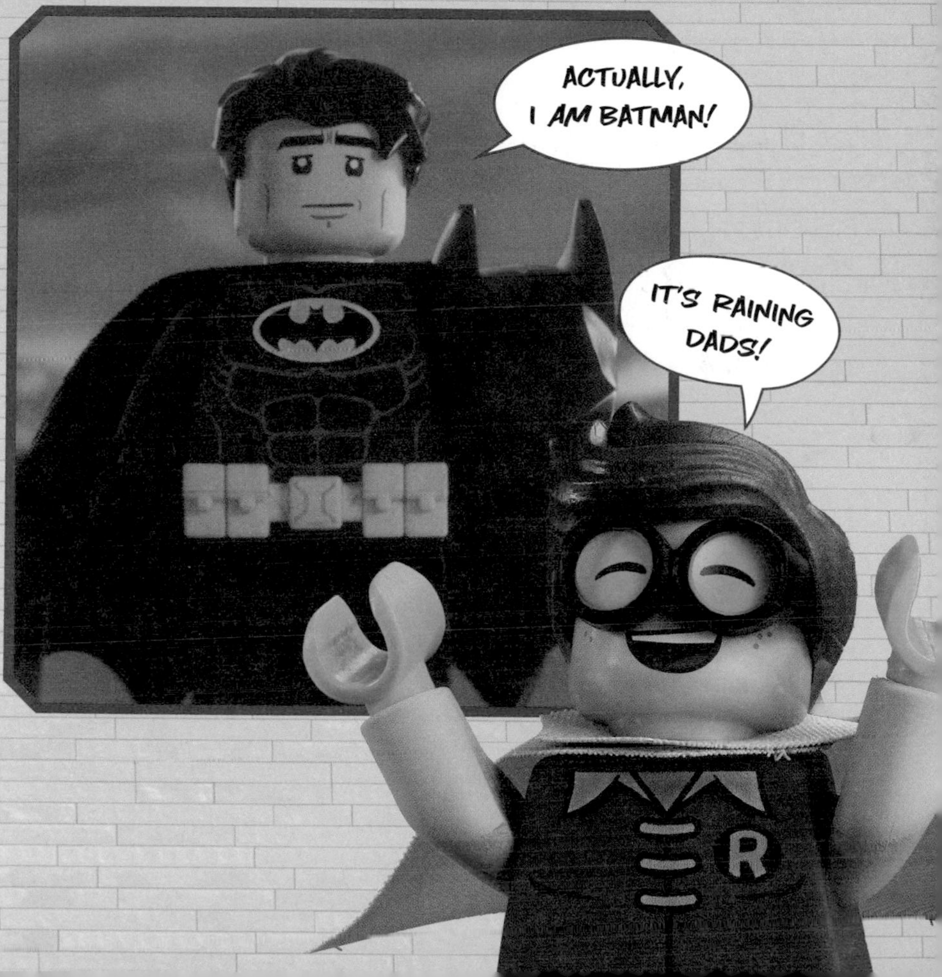
ACTUALLY, I AM BATMAN!
IT'S RAINING DADS!

ME AND MY DAD(S)'S FATHER FIGURE

After Bruce Wayne adopted me, I met Alfred. He's my dad's kind-of, sort-of dad. He's not really Bruce Wayne's dad. But Bruce/Batman thinks of him as a dad. So I guess that makes him my granddad. Cool!

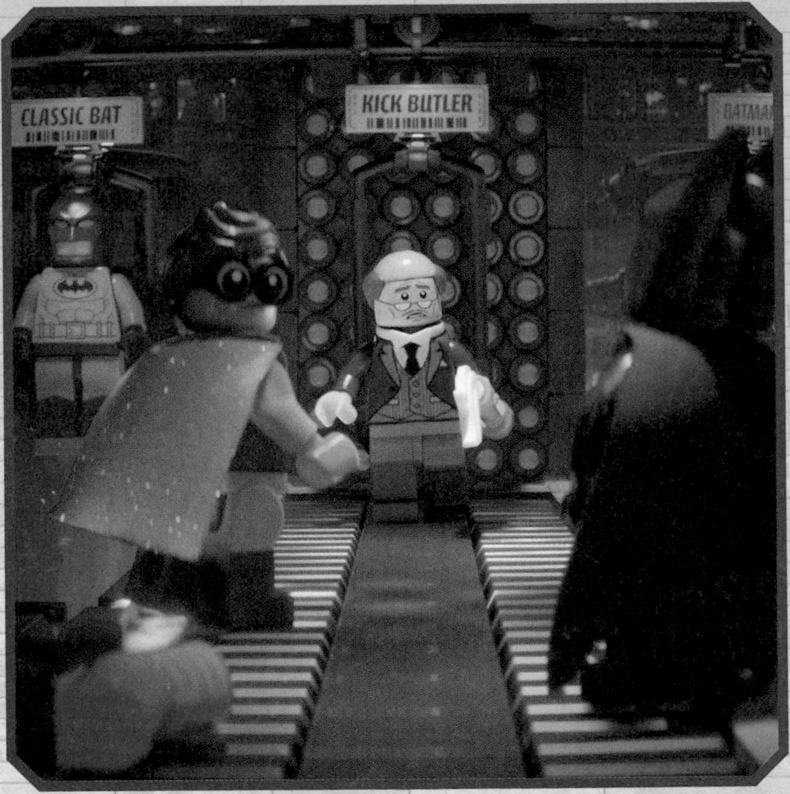
CLASSIC BAT
KICK BUTLER

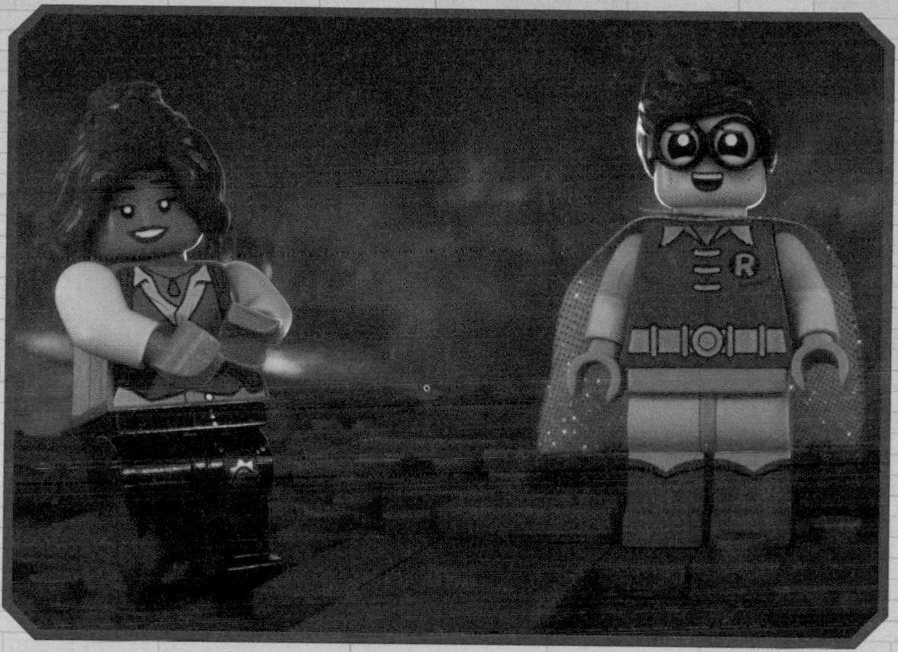
R

ME AND MY DAD(S)'S CRIME-FIGHTING BUDDY

And this is Barbara Gordon, the new police commissioner of Gotham City. She doesn't mess around. She even learned Brazilian jiujitsu at Harvard for Police. Anyone who knows how to fight crime in Gotham City like my dad Batman is A-OK in my book!

LIFE IS COOL(ER) WITH FAMILY

With my new family, I learned all kinds of ways to be cool(er) than ever before. And that's what I'm going to teach you!

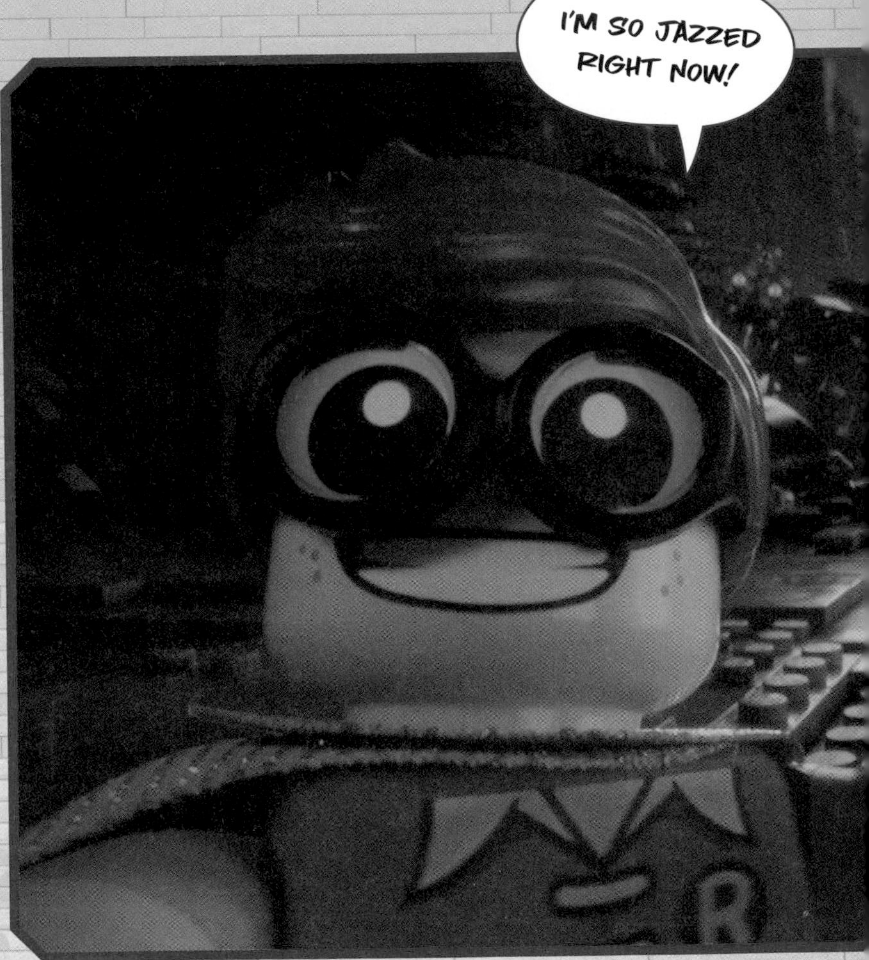
I'M SO JAZZED RIGHT NOW!

Just wait and see—there are going to be costumes and catchphrases, maybe even a song or two. I know I can't wait. Let's get grooving!

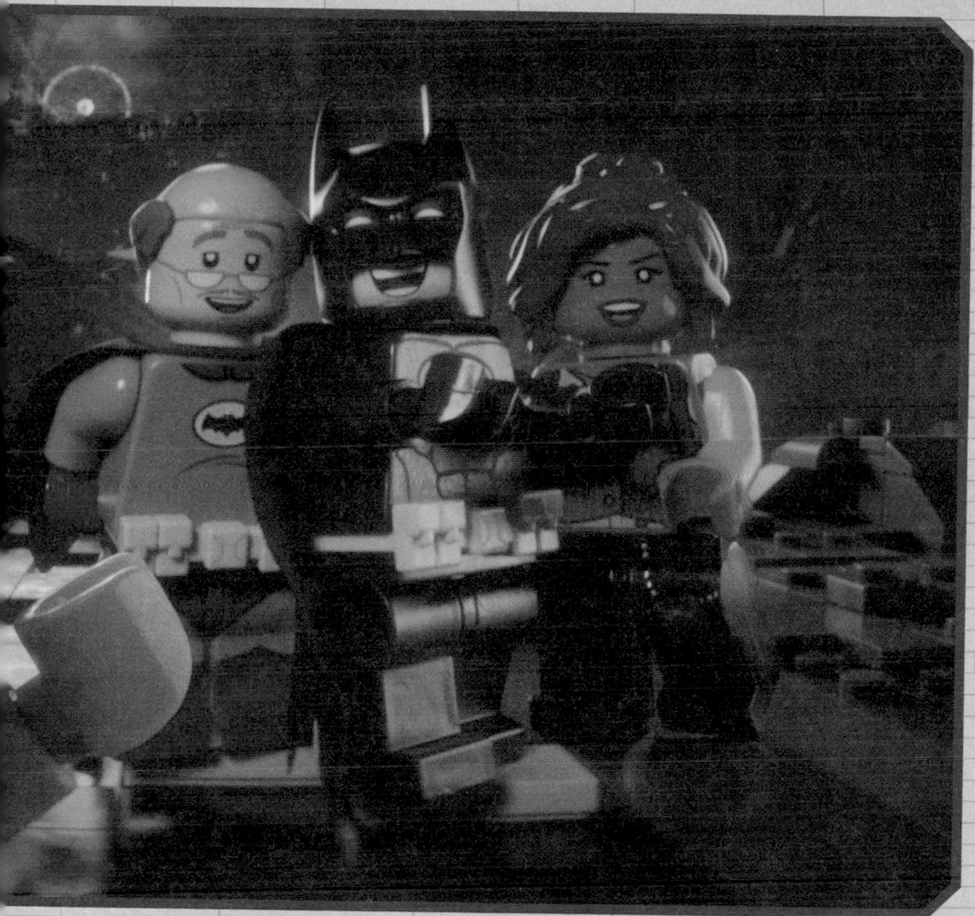

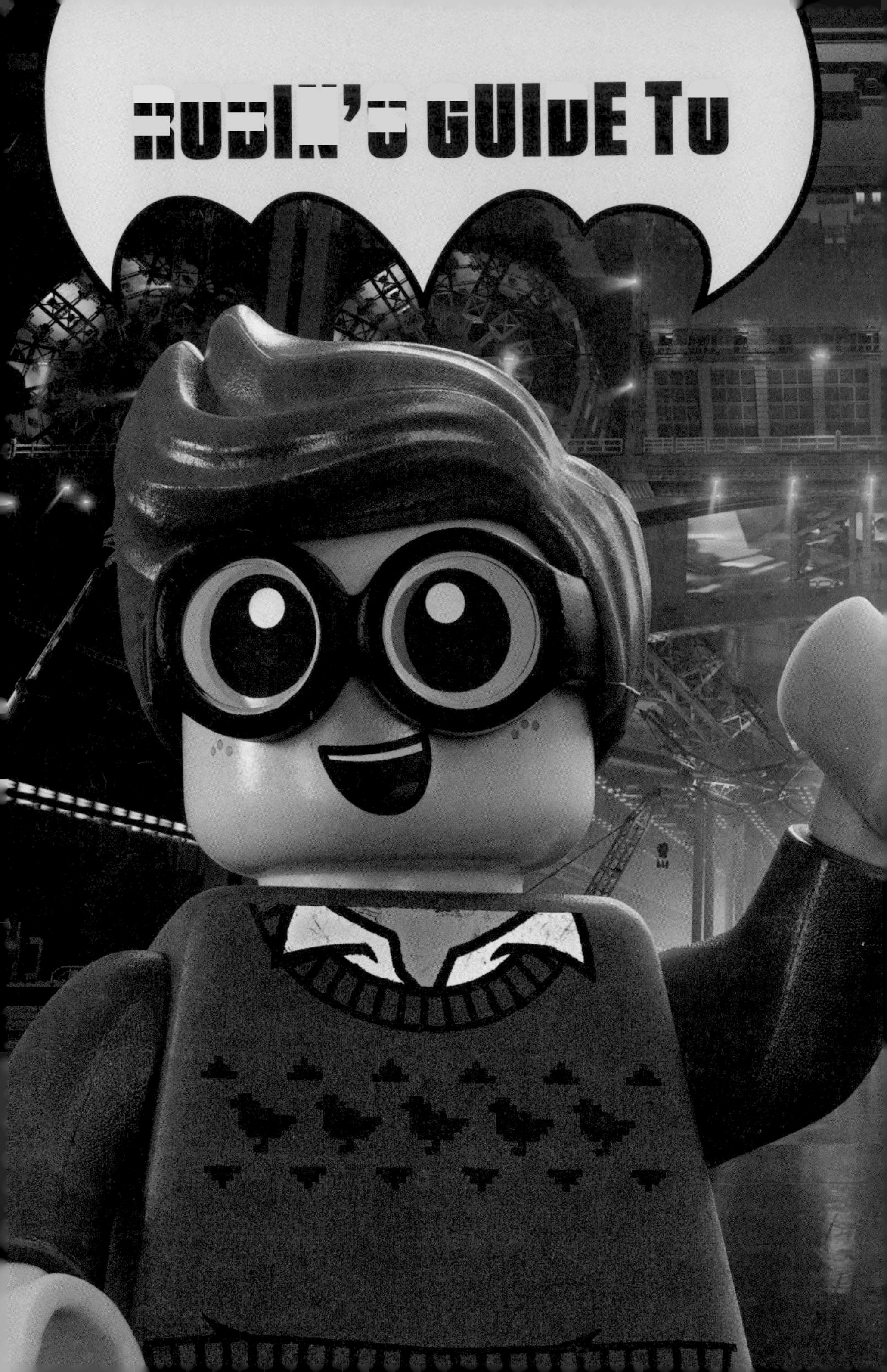
ROBIN'S GUIDE TO

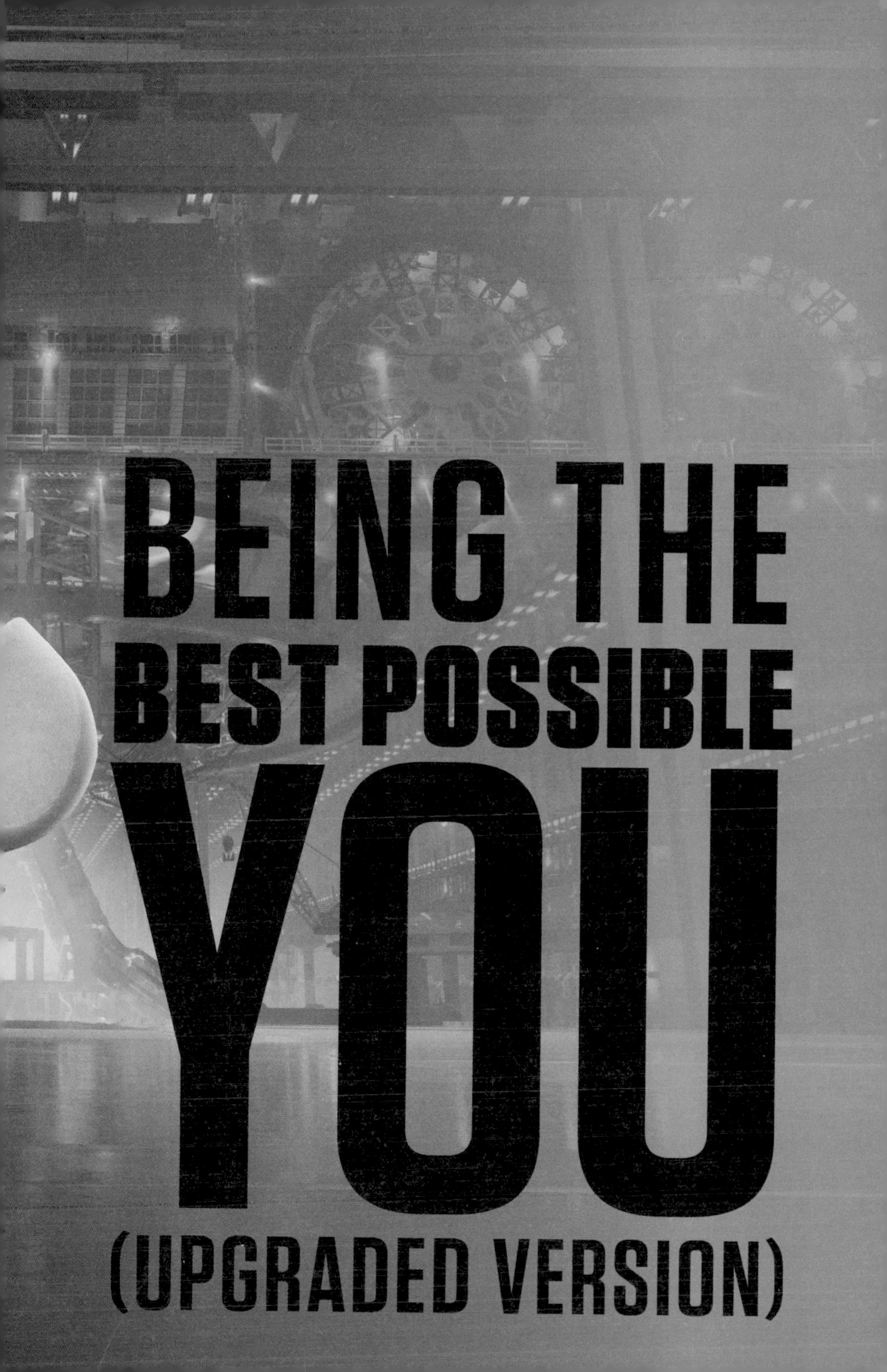

BEING THE BEST POSSIBLE YOU (UPGRADED VERSION)

THE UPGRADED YOU

The best way to be cool(er) is to be the best possible you. And the only way to do that is by constantly making personal improvements. How do I know? Well, let's just say I've been working on a few upgrades of my own.

When I was at the orphanage, I had lots of time to focus on self-improvement. The usual stuff: yoga, meditating, deep-sea welding. And boy, did it come in handy. Those "upgrades" were *exactly* what Mr. Wayne was looking for in an adopted son!

UPGRADE #1:

Teeth whitener. Pearly whites as bright as light!

UPGRADE #2:

Large, vulnerable-looking eyes. It takes a while to perfect the "puppy-dog" stare. I used to practice in the mirror for eight hours a day.

UPGRADE #3:

Mad cooking skills. The way to your *padre*'s heart is through his stomach!

UPGRADE #4:

Close-up street magic. I can be very mysterious when I desire to be.

IT'S WHAT'S INSIDE THAT COUNTS

But once Mr. Wayne adopted me and I started going on missions with him as Batman and Robin (shhhh!), I realized that the best upgrades aren't the ones you make on the outside. They're the ones you make on the inside that count, like being courageous, having heart, and always bringing the upbeat beats to the party!

ARE YOU READY TO TAKE ON THE JOKER?

I'M DOWN TO STOP THAT CLOWN!

My *padre* was super impressed by my unending enthusiasm.

Batman wasn't really into *feelings* when we first met. But I softened his heart with a big ol' H-U-G.

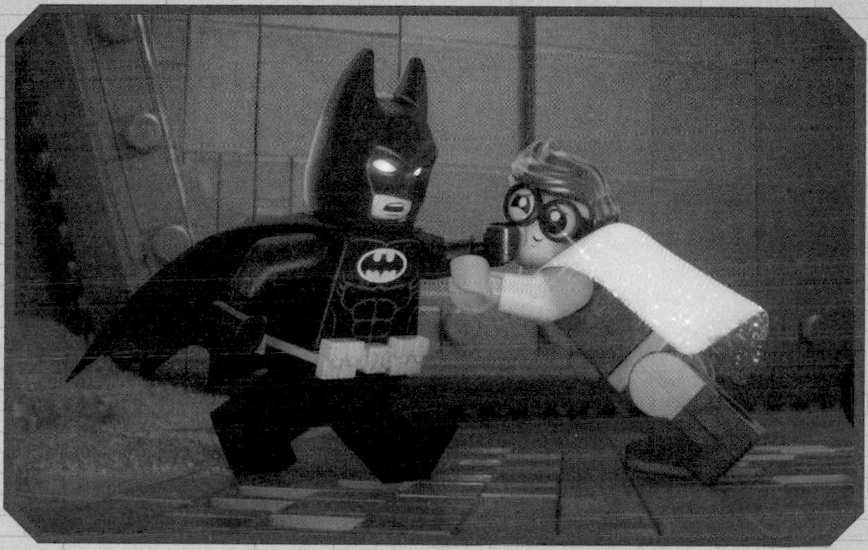

Plus, no one can resist my choice in Super Hero soundtrack tunes!

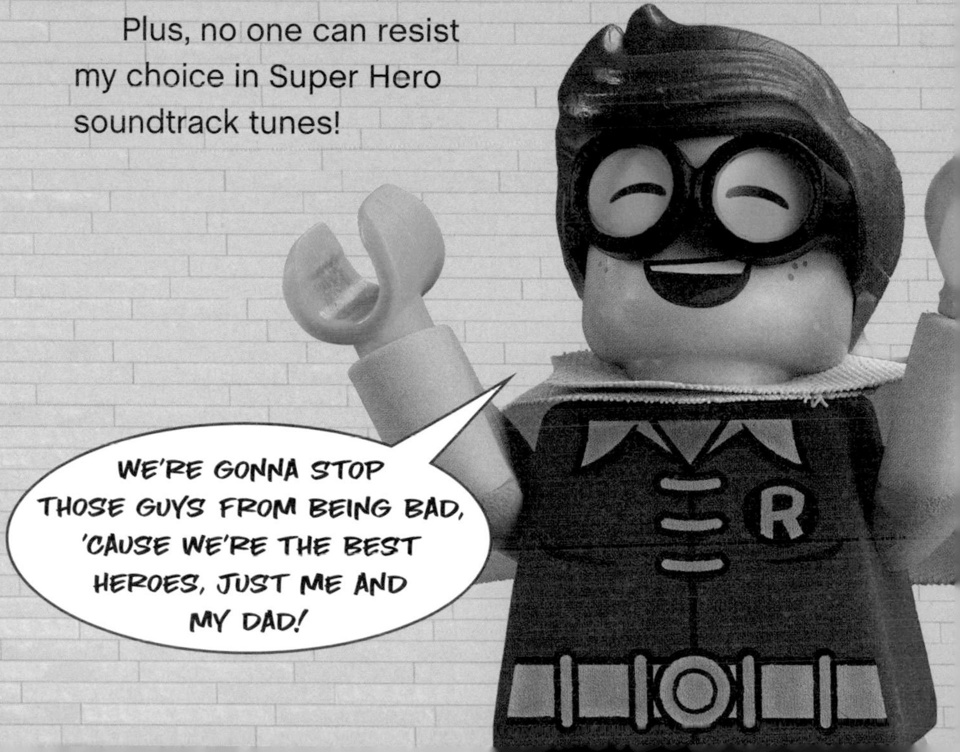
WE'RE GONNA STOP THOSE GUYS FROM BEING BAD, 'CAUSE WE'RE THE BEST HEROES, JUST ME AND MY DAD!
R

TRAINING HARDCORE

Of course, being the best possible you doesn't come easy. You need to train hard to achieve your goals, whether you're working toward good grades, playing sports, or perfecting your latest training routine.

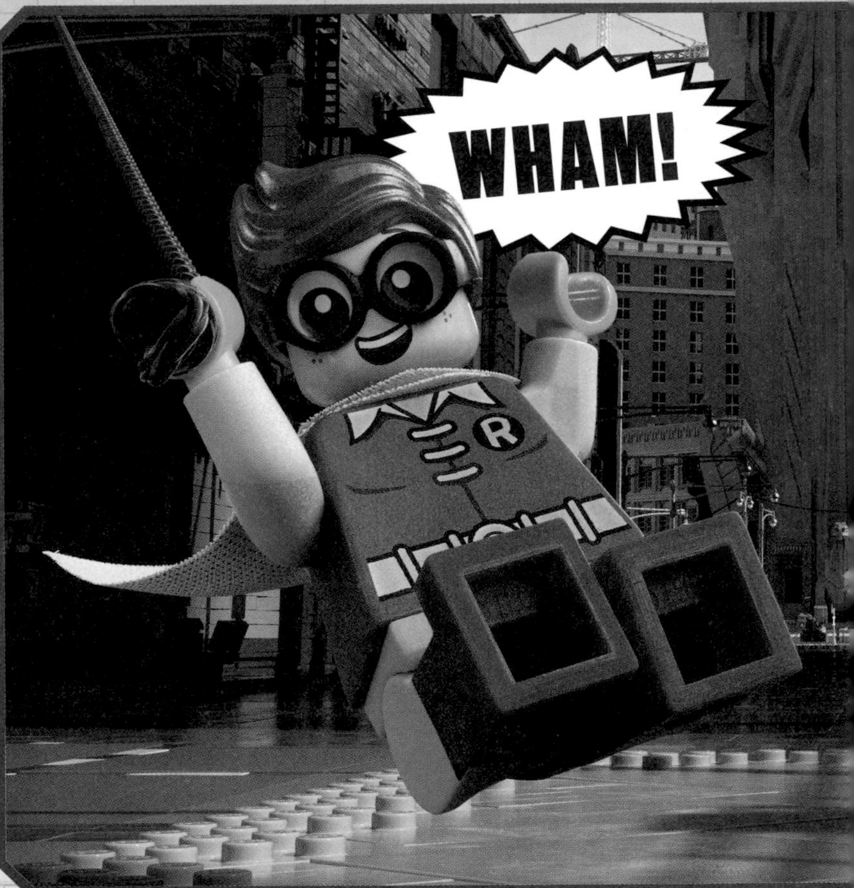
WHAM!

Like my old man says, being a Super Hero means working 24/7, 365, at a million percent.

This bad guy didn't know that I've been training in the gymnastics-based martial arts known as gymkata my whole life.

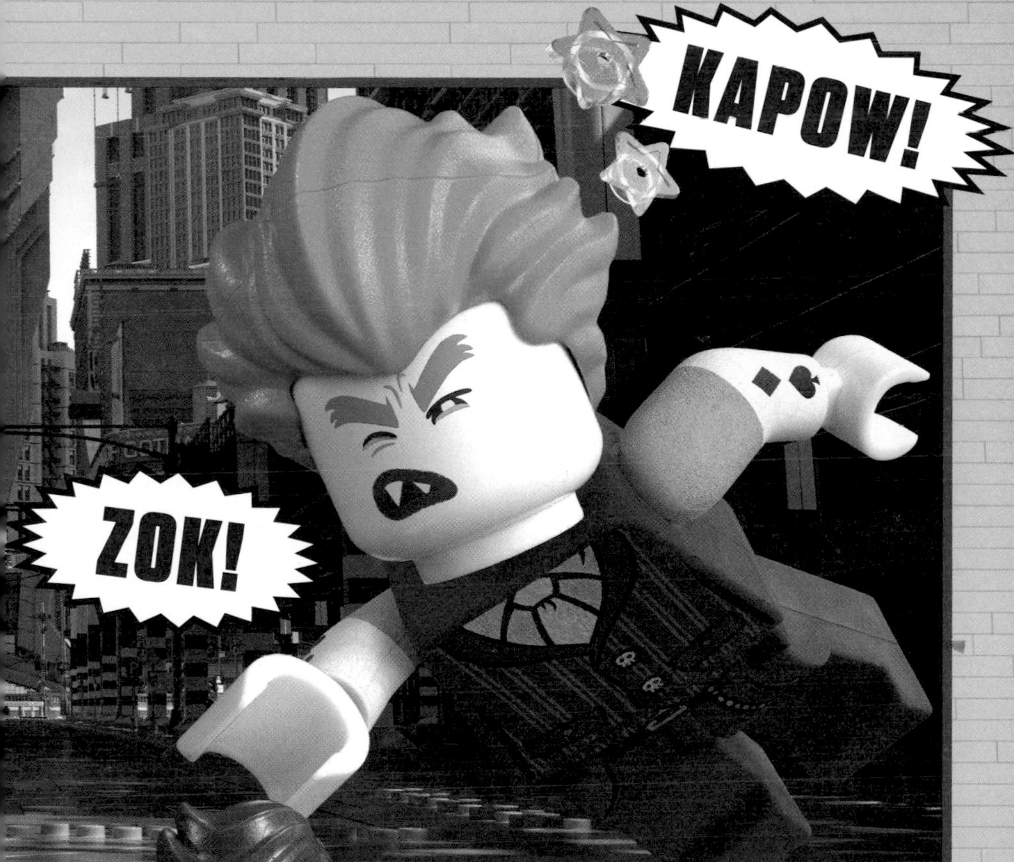
KAPOW!
ZOK!

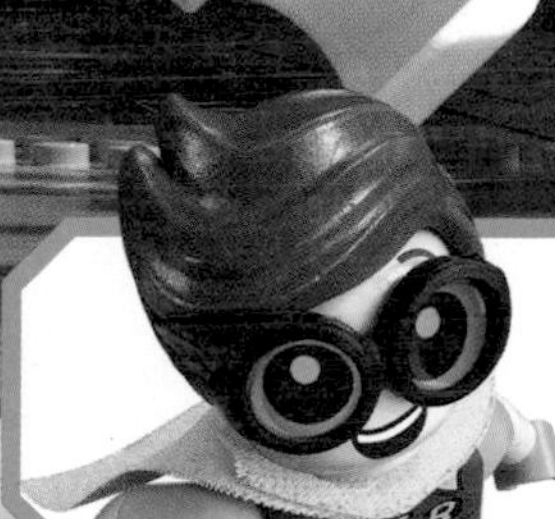

When was a time you trained really hard for something important?

CATCHING YOUR BIG BREAK

Knowing when to put all your self-improvements, inner upgrades, and hard training into action is key to being cool(er). In fact, I wouldn't be here teaching you how to be cool(er) if I hadn't been on the lookout for my big break. When I spotted Bruce Wayne at that fancy party, I knew I only had one shot to show him I was the son he never knew he needed.

STEP 1:
Acquire target.

THERE'S MR. WAYNE!

STEP 2:

Impress target with cool(er) upgrades.

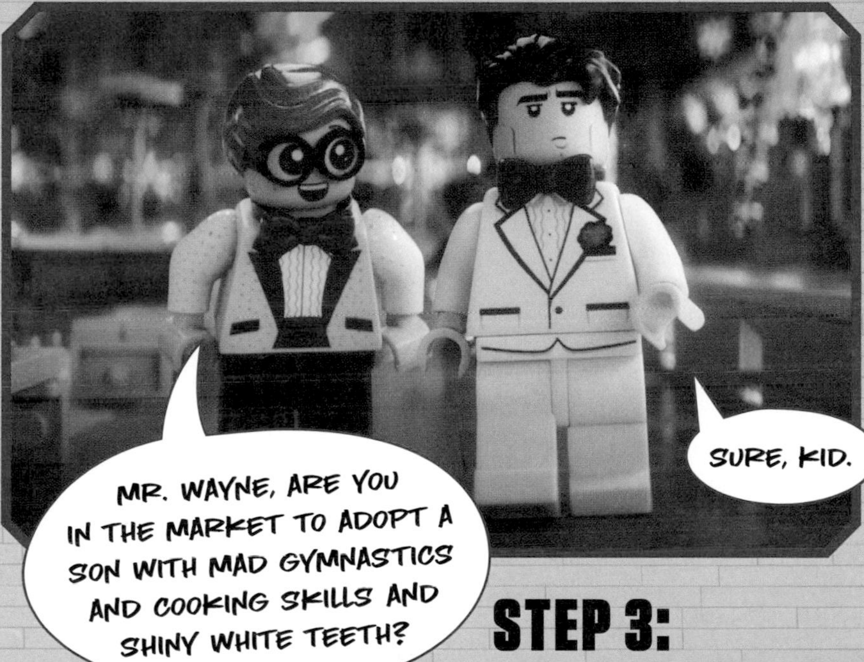
MR. WAYNE, ARE YOU IN THE MARKET TO ADOPT A SON WITH MAD GYMNASTICS AND COOKING SKILLS AND SHINY WHITE TEETH?
SURE, KID.

STEP 3:

Big break officially caught!

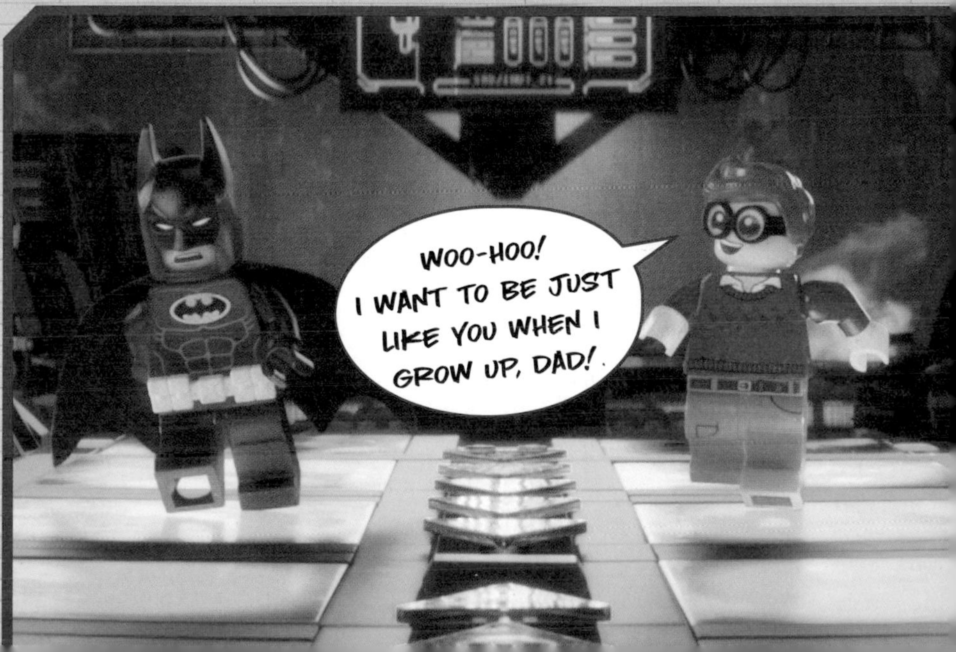
WOO-HOO! I WANT TO BE JUST LIKE YOU WHEN I GROW UP, DAD!

HOW TO TELL IF YOU'VE ACHIEVED MAXIMUM UPGRADE

Oh my gosh, it's quiz time! I love quizzes. They're a great way to learn things about yourself *you didn't even know were there.*

So let's get grooving. Have you achieved your own maximum level of upgraded-ness? Answer these questions to find out if you're blah or TA-DA!

1. Do you have unique hobbies that make you stand out in the crowd? Sample hobbies include water aerobics, driftwood art, and beatboxing.

2. Can you speak a foreign language, like Danish or Tagalog?

3. Do you have a code name?

4. When you smile, do people mistake your shiny white teeth for the sun?

5. Are your eyes particularly large and vulnerable-looking?

6. Do people find your enthusiasm contagious?

7. When your friends or family need help, are you there on the double?

8. Have you ever worked hard to achieve something you thought might be impossible?

9. Do you have big dreams that you aren't afraid to go after?

10. Is your dad Batman?

*If you answered "yes" to five or more questions, congratulations! You've achieved maximum upgrade.

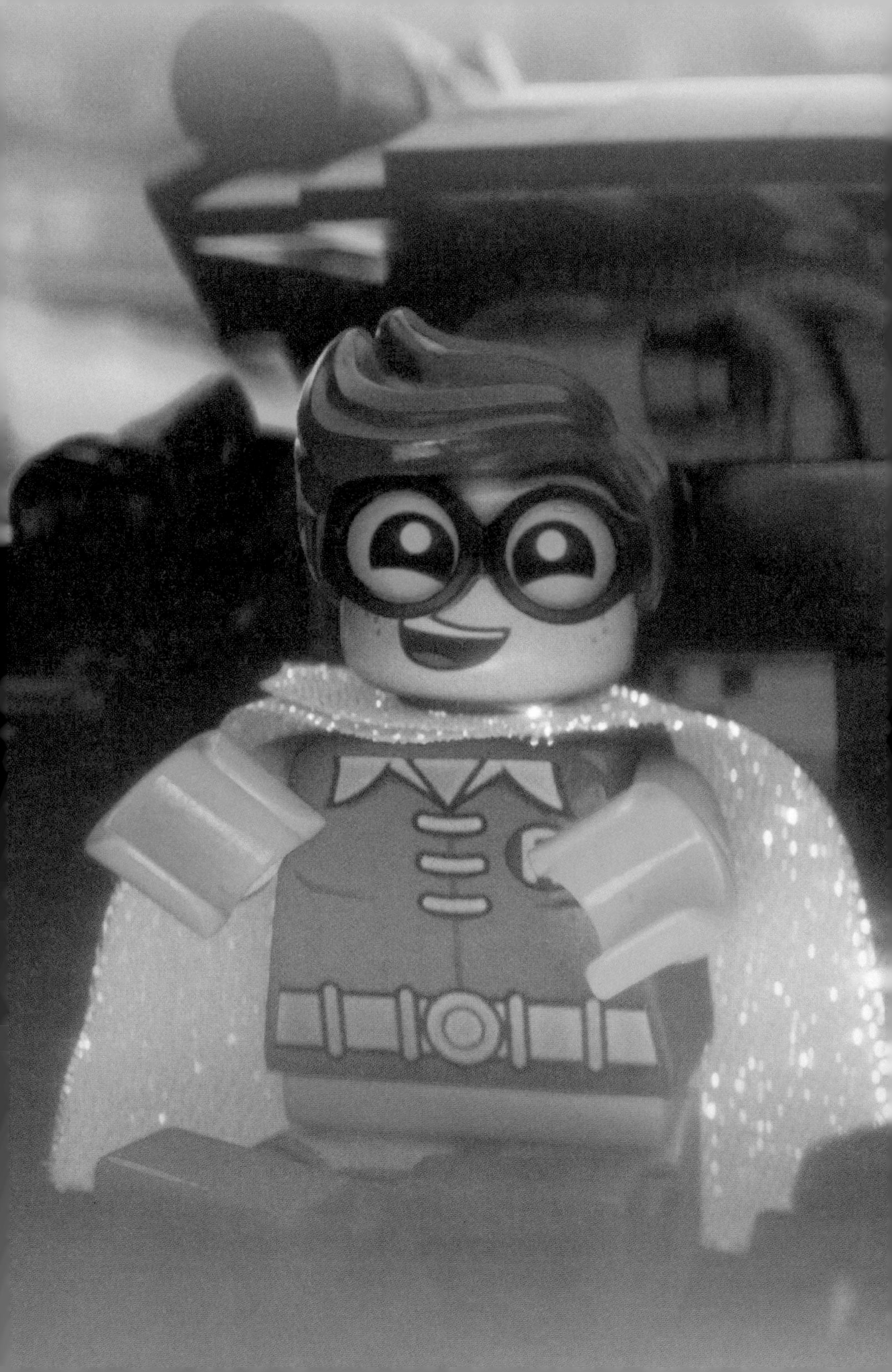

COOL(ER) LIFE LESSON #1:

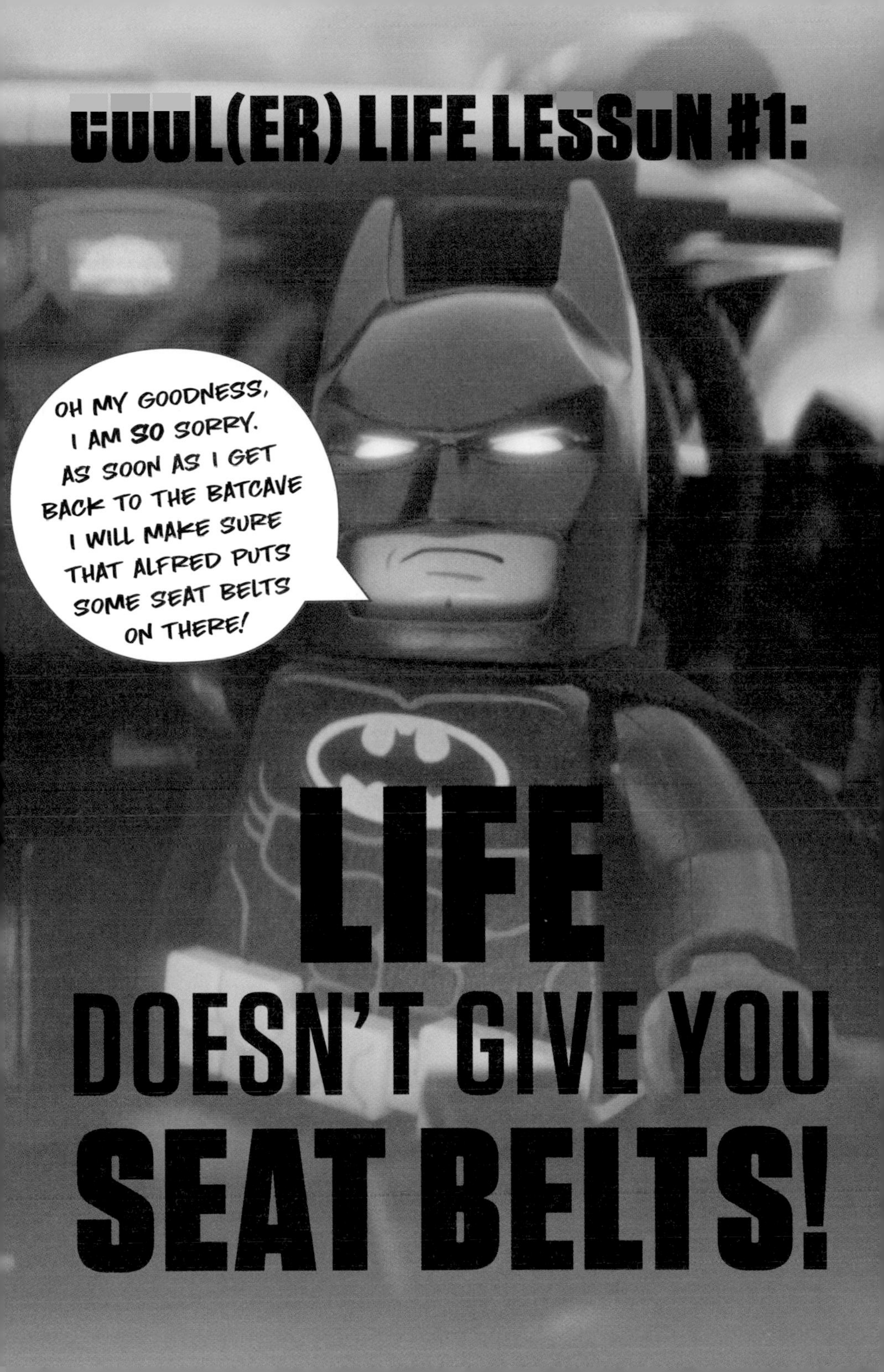

LIFE DOESN'T GIVE YOU SEAT BELTS!

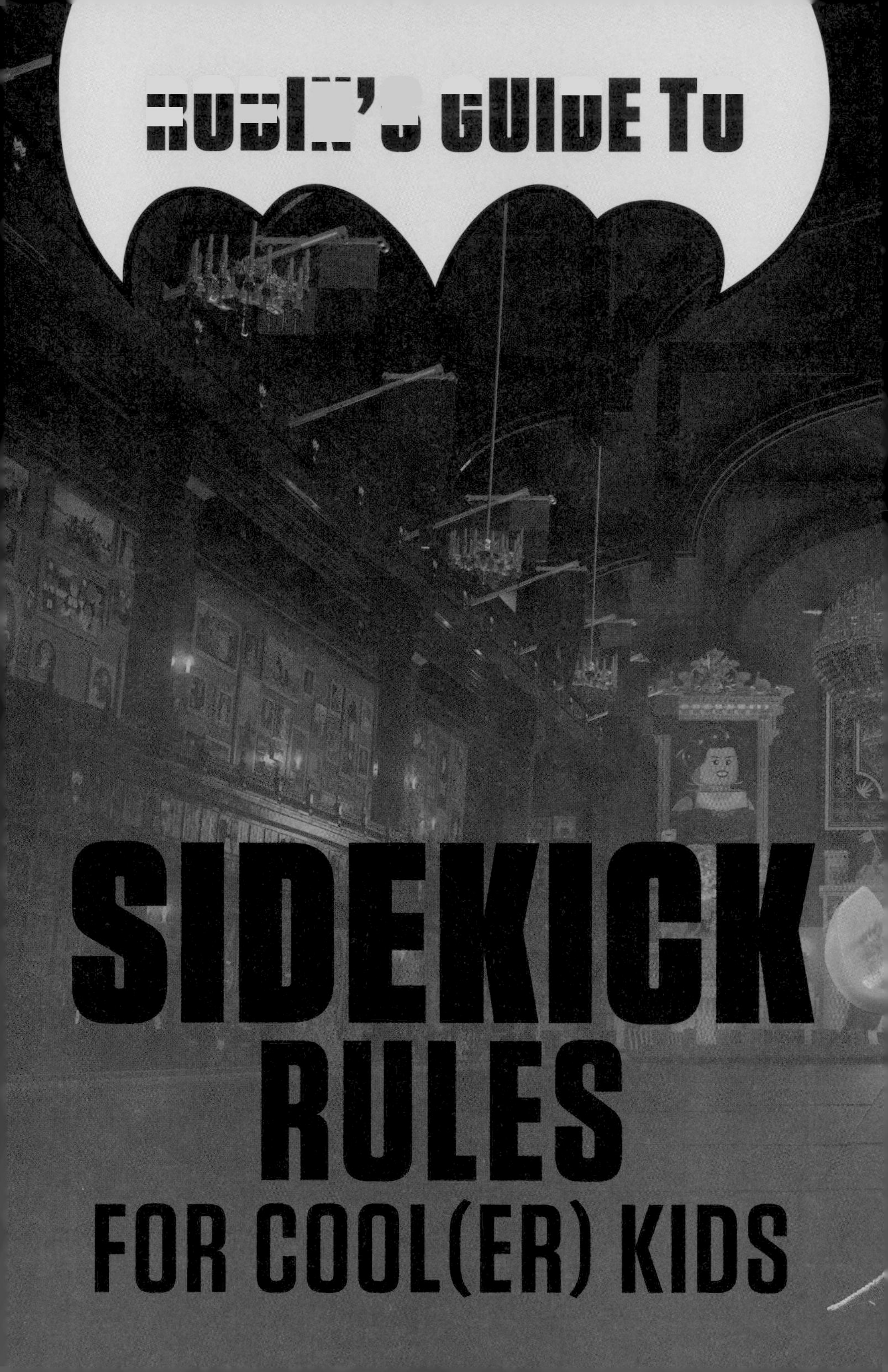
ROBIN'S GUIDE TO
SIDEKICK
RULES
FOR COOL(ER) KIDS

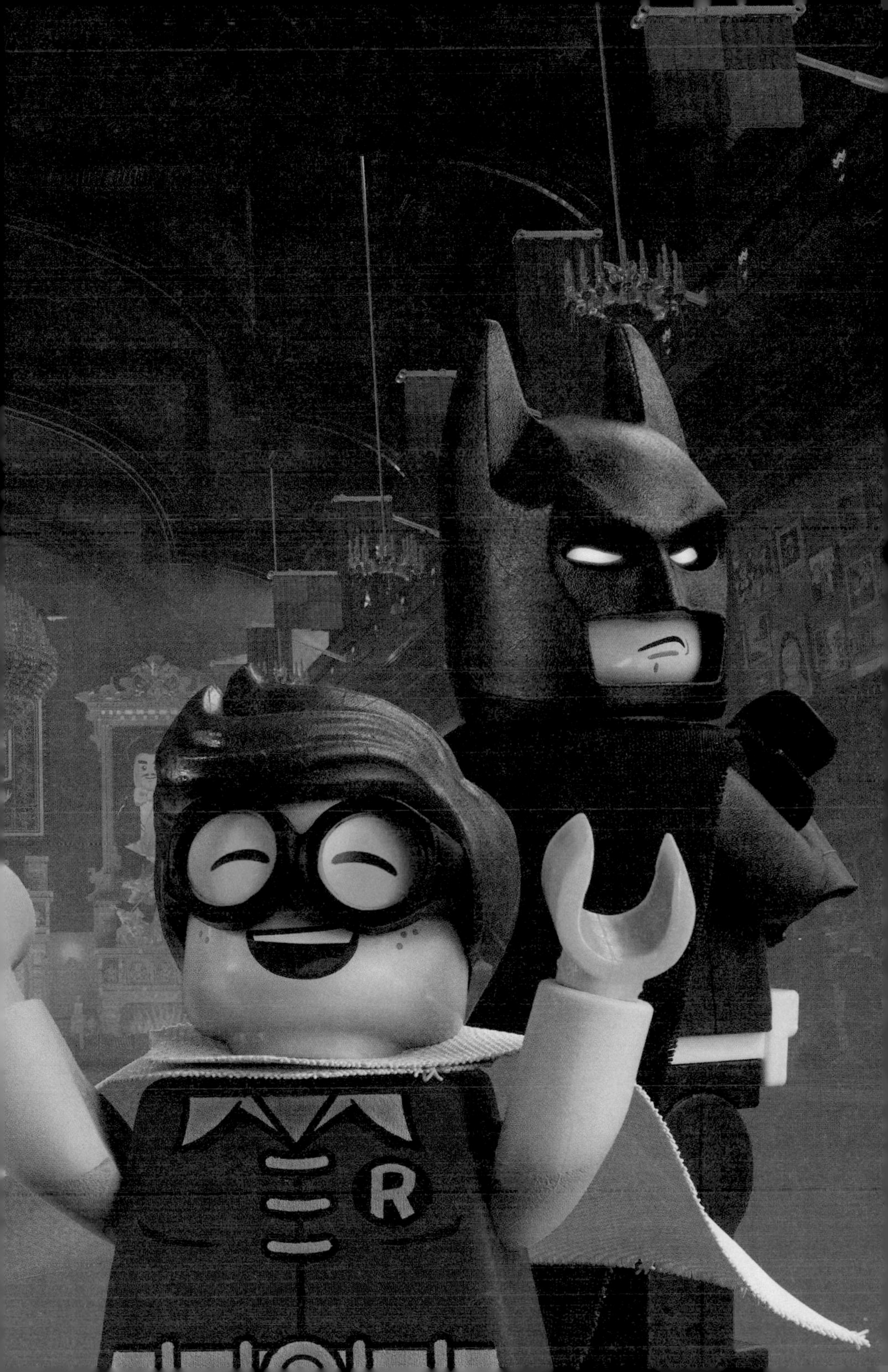

ALWAYS FOLLOW YOUR HERO'S LEAD

Sometimes being cool(er) means following the rules. It may not sound cool, but when you're a sidekick (like me), and you have a totally awesome dad like Batman (he's my *padre*), then it's especially important to follow the rules. Otherwise you might end up trapped in an atomic cauldron. Or laser-zapped by a Kryptonian defense system. Or both.

SIDEKICK RULE #1:

Employ excellent listening skills and execution of Super Hero ideas.

DROP TO THE GROUND!

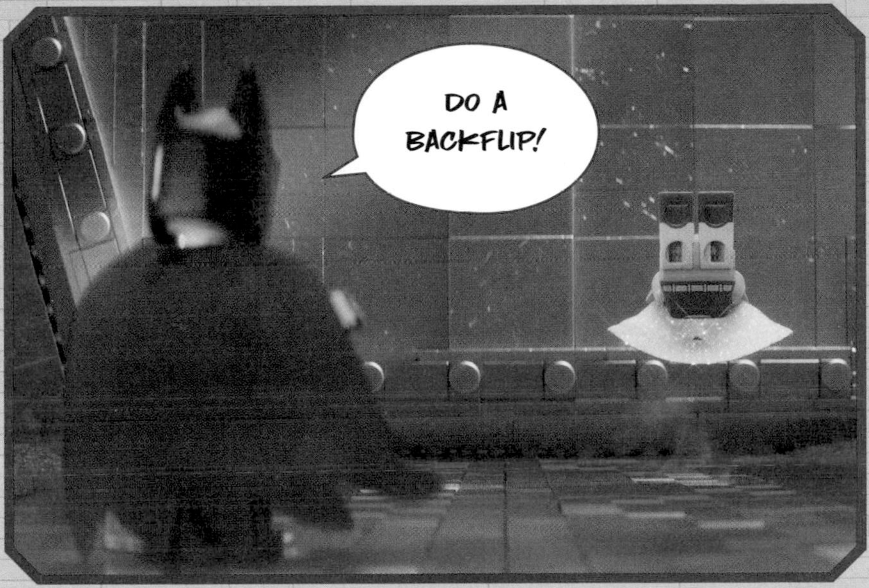
DO A BACKFLIP!

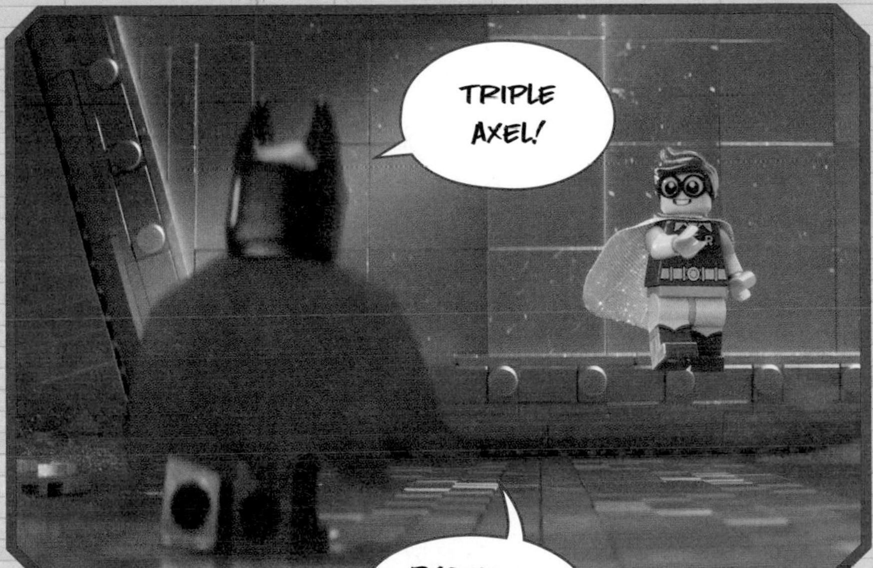
TRIPLE AXEL!
EXCELLENT LISTENING!

SIDEKICK RULE #2:

Always ask your parents for permission before going on a stealth mission to a rival hero's secret base on a frozen tundra.

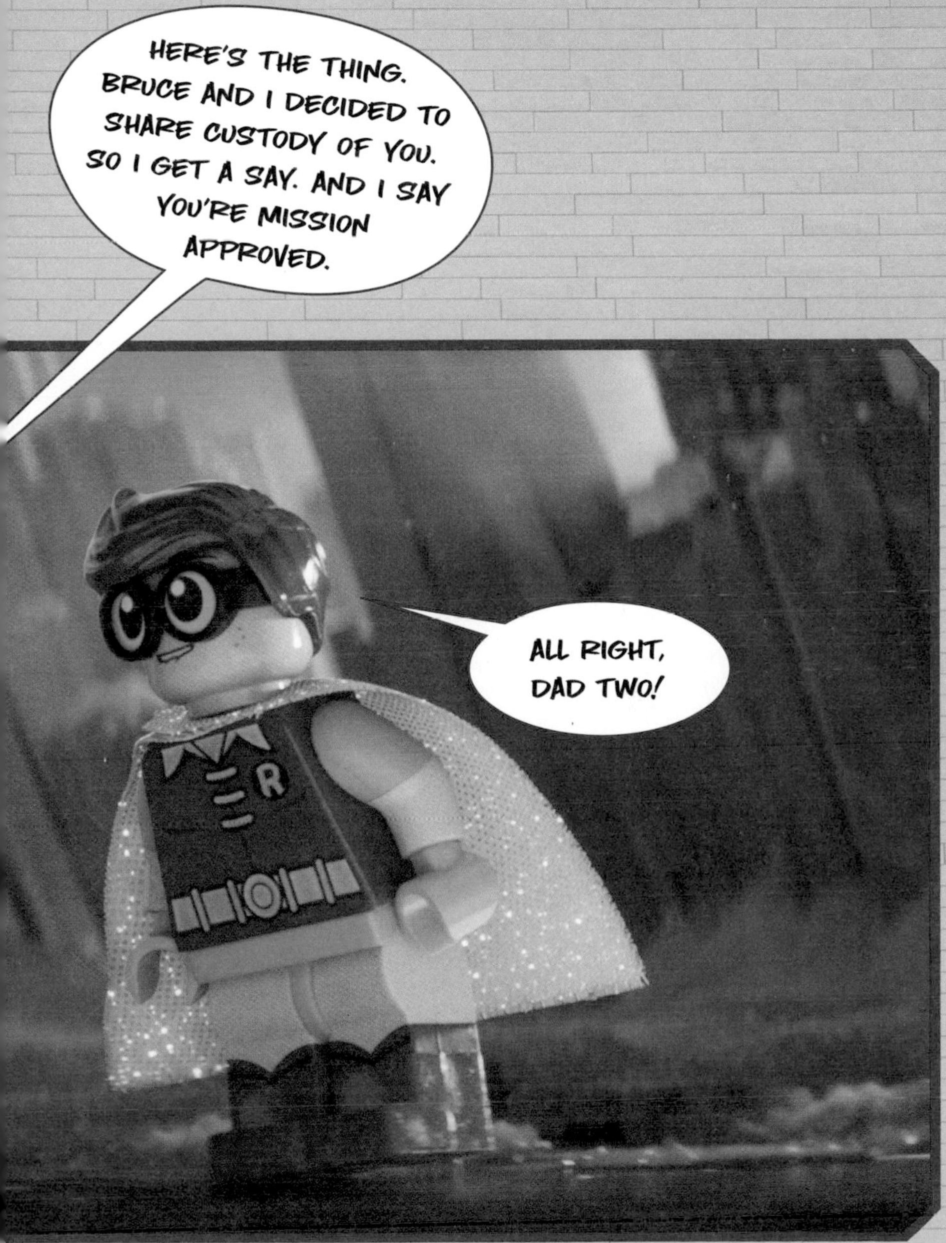
HERE'S THE THING. BRUCE AND I DECIDED TO SHARE CUSTODY OF YOU. SO I GET A SAY. AND I SAY YOU'RE MISSION APPROVED.
ALL RIGHT, DAD TWO!

SIDEKICK RULE #3:

Stick it out with your Super Hero mentor, no matter how bad things get.

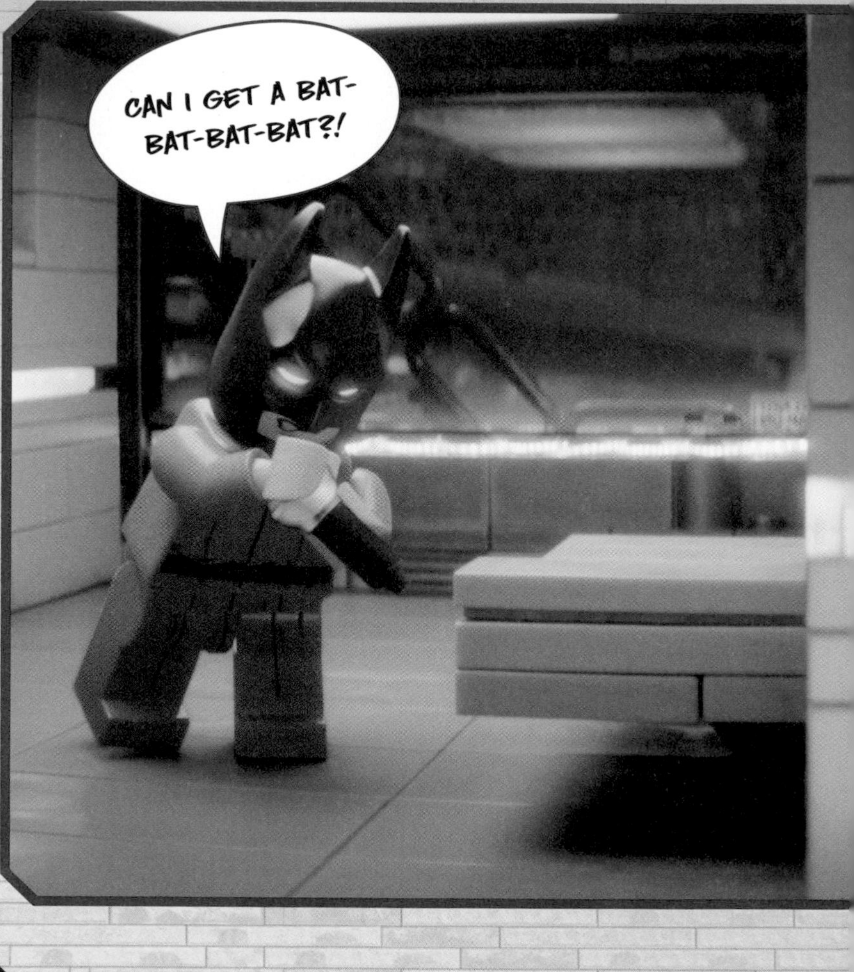
CAN I GET A BAT-BAT-BAT-BAT?!

When Batman was thrown into Arkham Asylum for sending the Joker to the Phantom Zone, did I leave his side? Heck no! I was right there with him in the pokey, and we made it through the tough times by beatboxing our woes away. Now *that's* cool(er)!

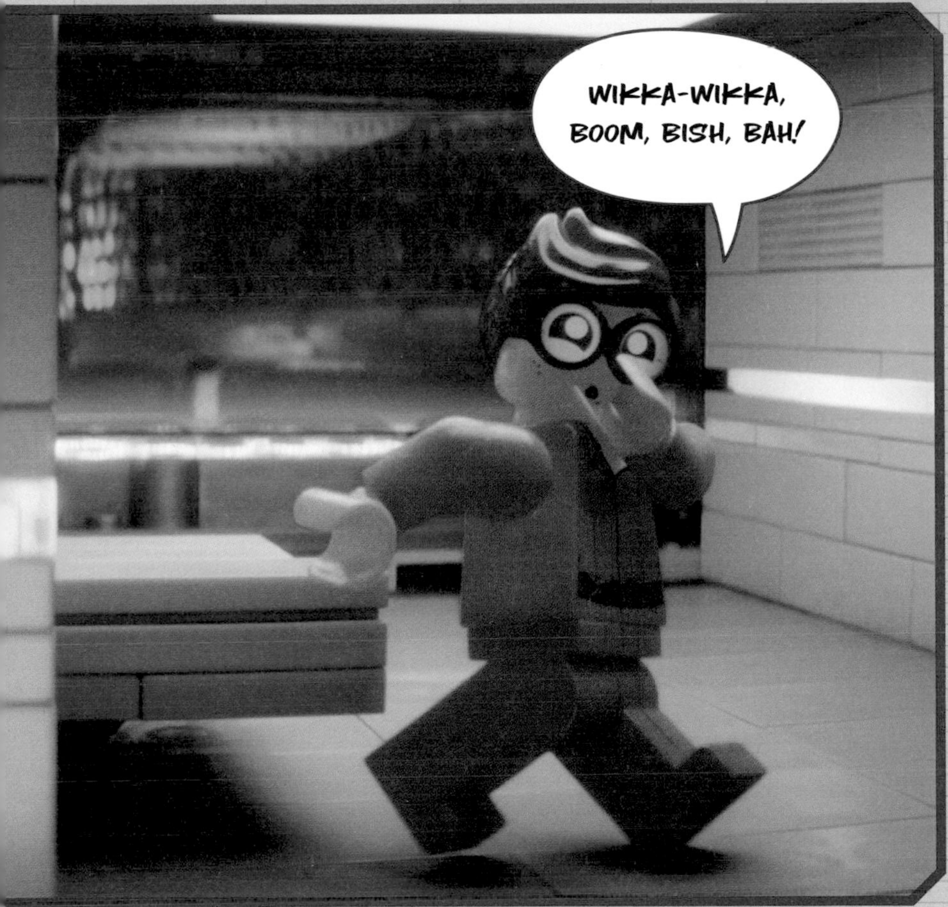
WIKKA-WIKKA, BOOM, BISH, BAH!

QUIZ: SIDEKICK OR SUPER HERO?

Woo-hoo! Quiz time again. Answer these questions to see if you're a kick-butt sidekick or a super-duper Super Hero.

1. Are you good at following instructions? Or are you Batman?

2. Are you gymnastically inclined? Or are you Batman?

3. Do you dress in bright, vibrant colors? Or are you Batman?

4. Do you enjoy upbeat pop music? Or are you Batman?

5. Are you a normal human being? Or do you have a nine-pack, like Batman? (Yeah, that's right—my Mega-Cool dad has an extra ab!)

*Quiz Results: You are a sidekick. Unless you're Batman.

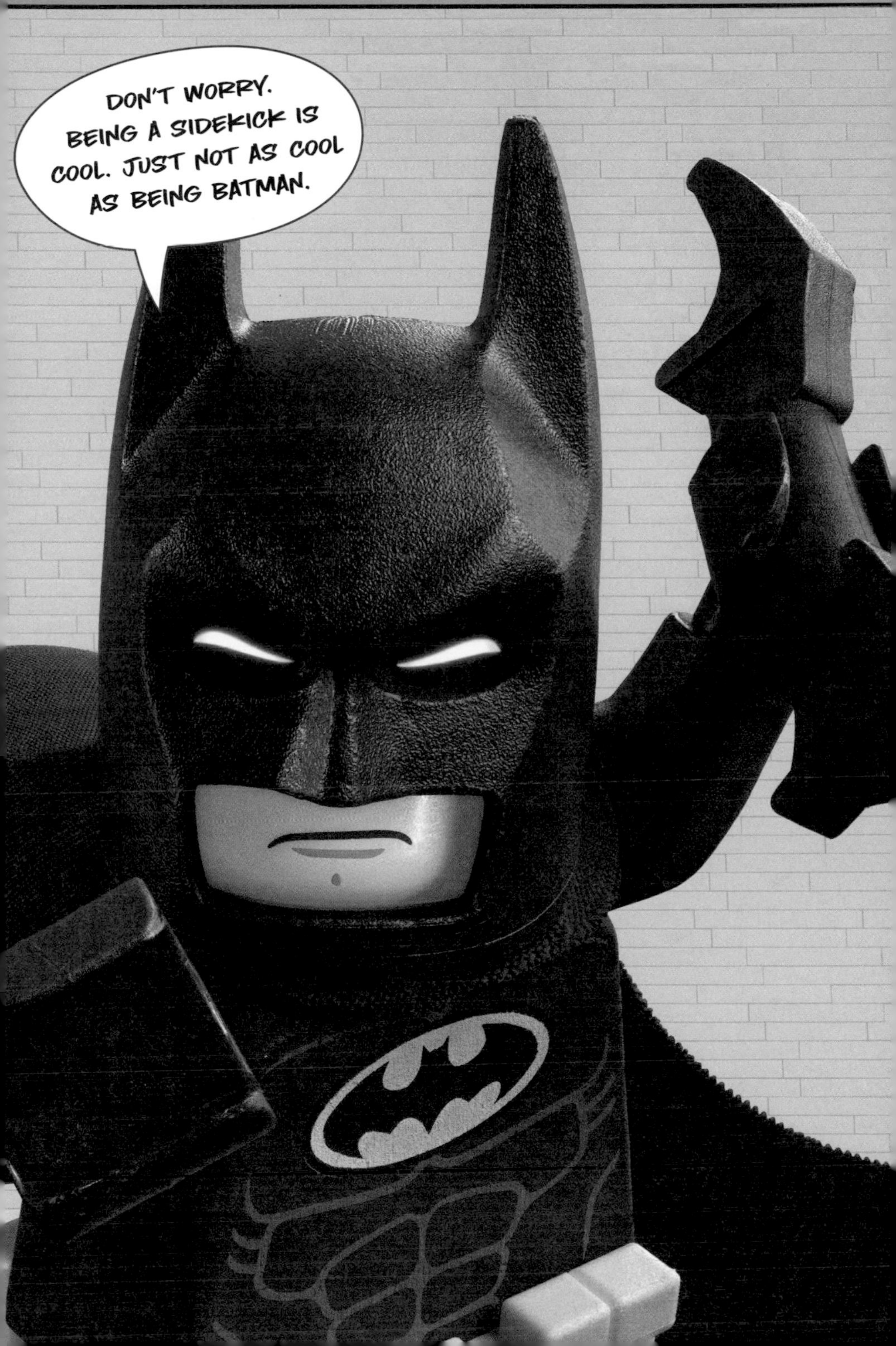
DON'T WORRY. BEING A SIDEKICK IS COOL. JUST NOT AS COOL AS BEING BATMAN.

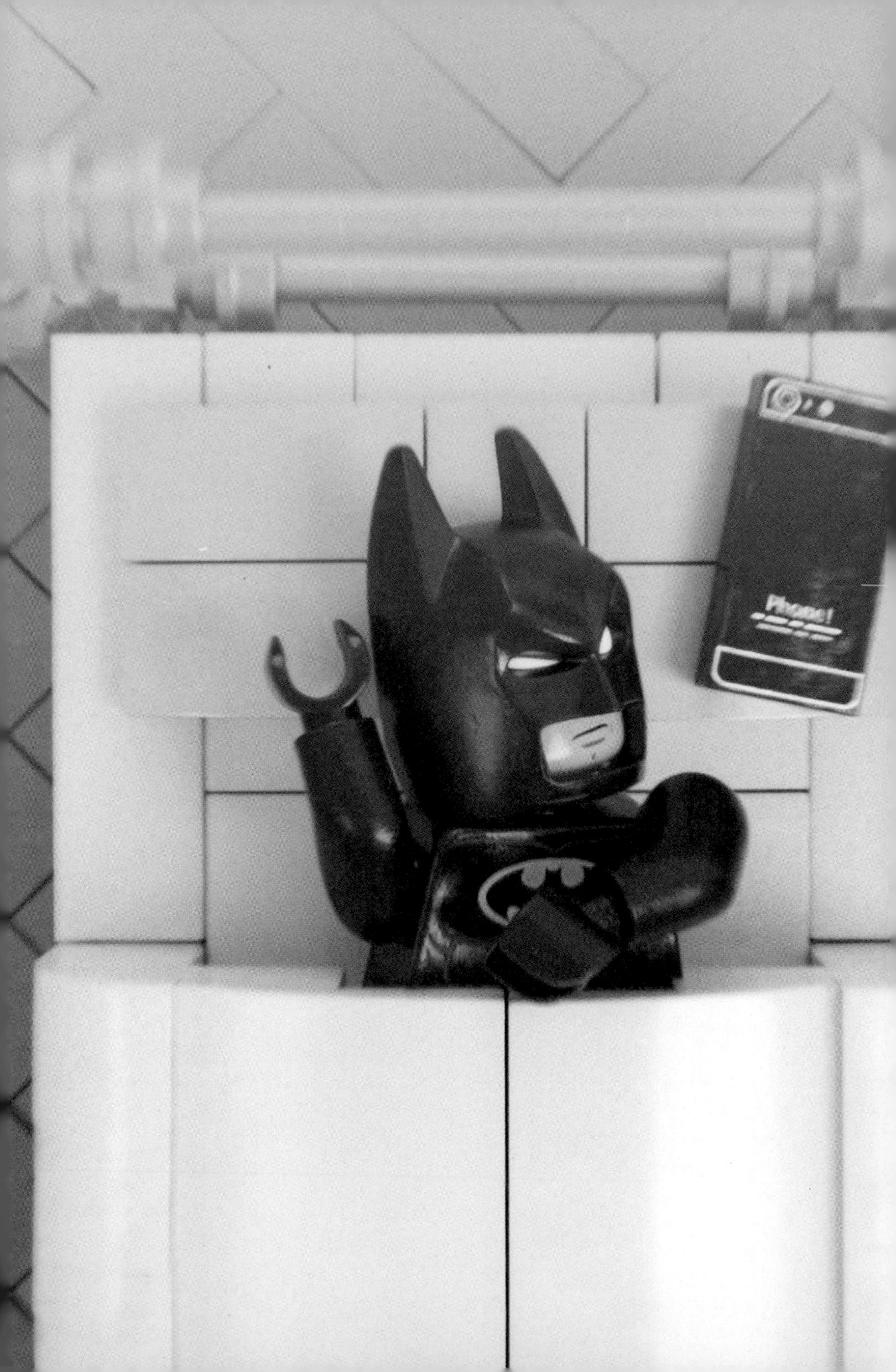
Phone!

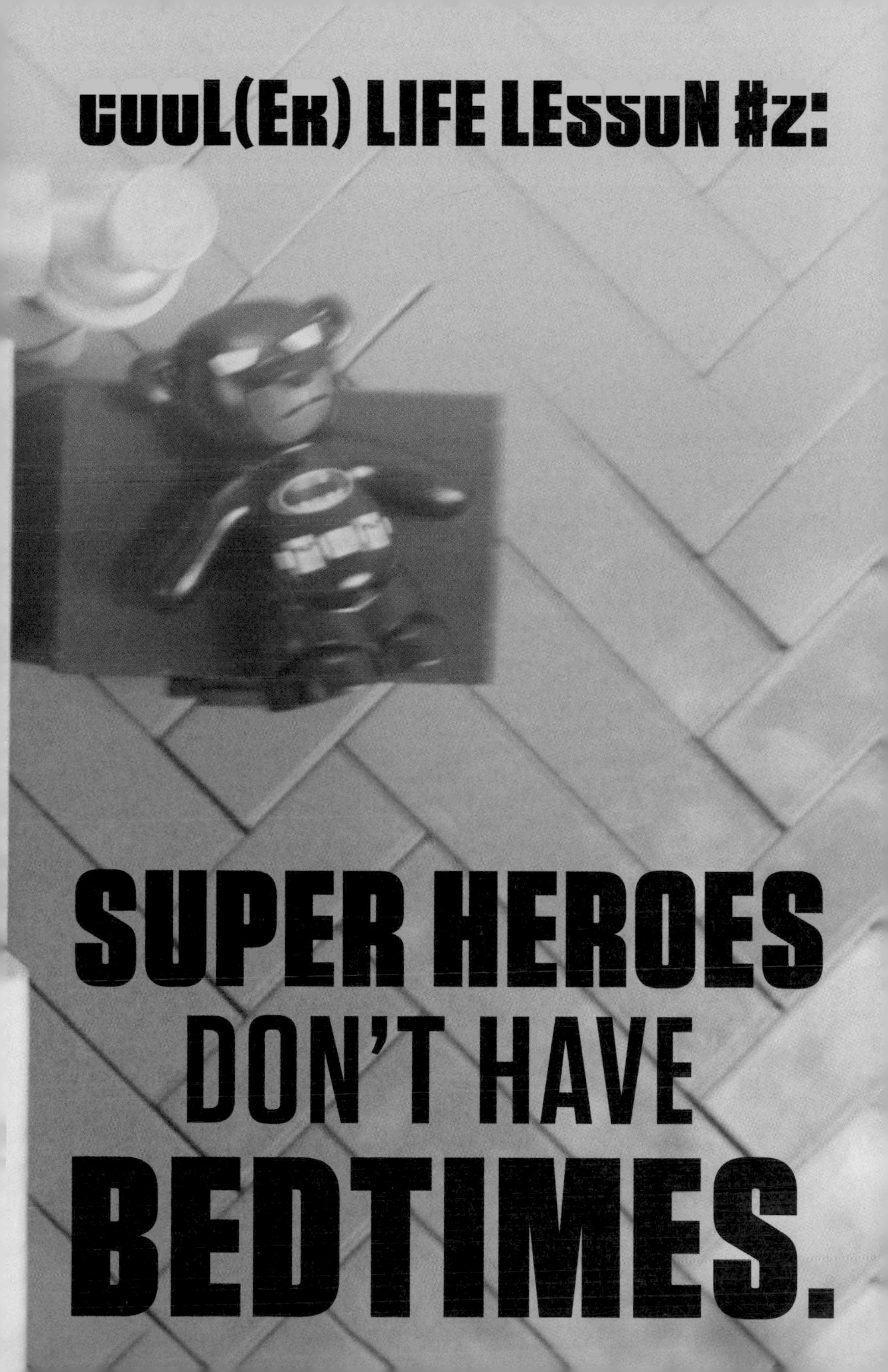

COOL(ER) LIFE LESSON #2:

SUPER HEROES DON'T HAVE BEDTIMES.

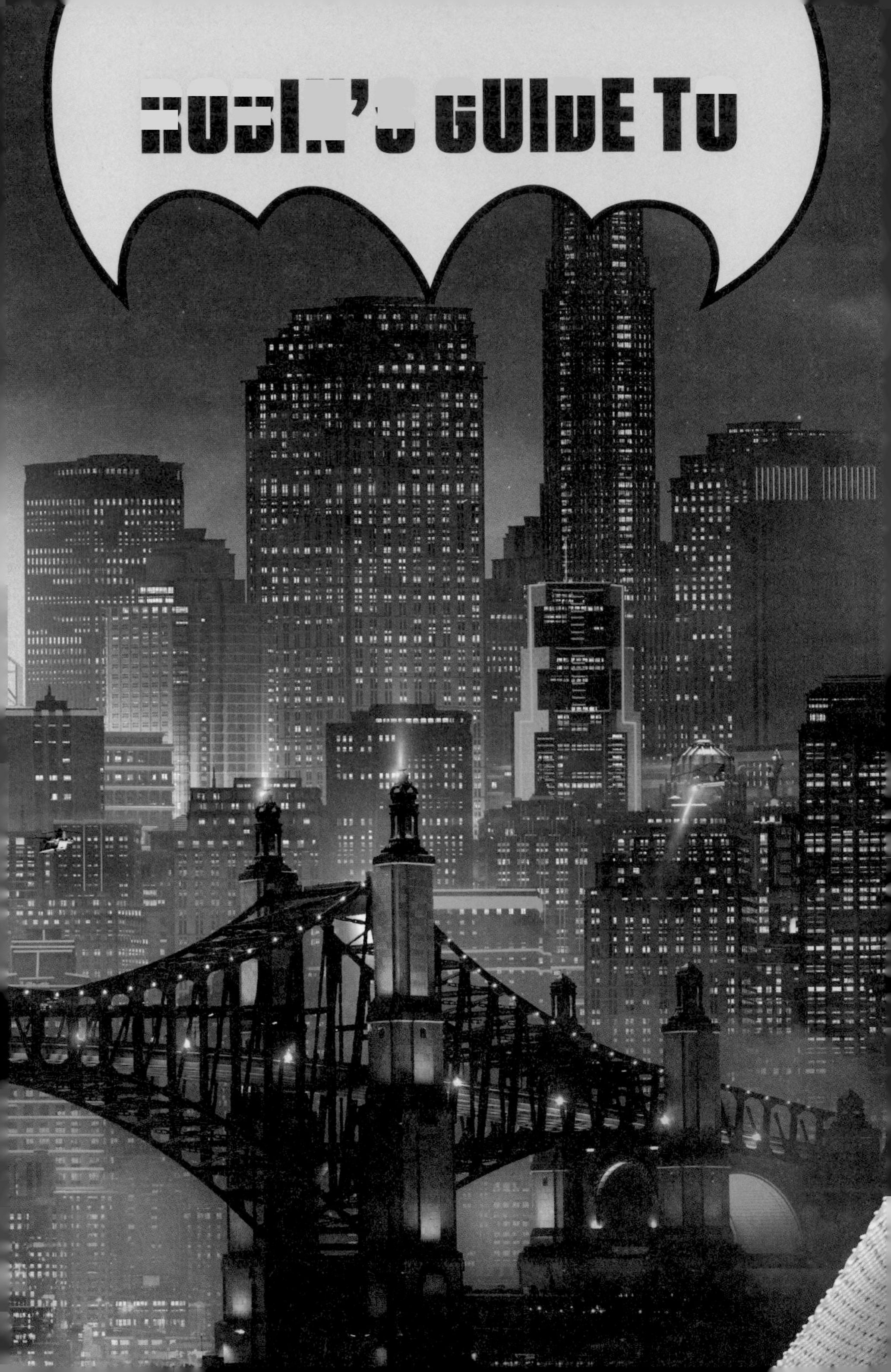
ROBIN'S GUIDE TO

DRESSING THE PART

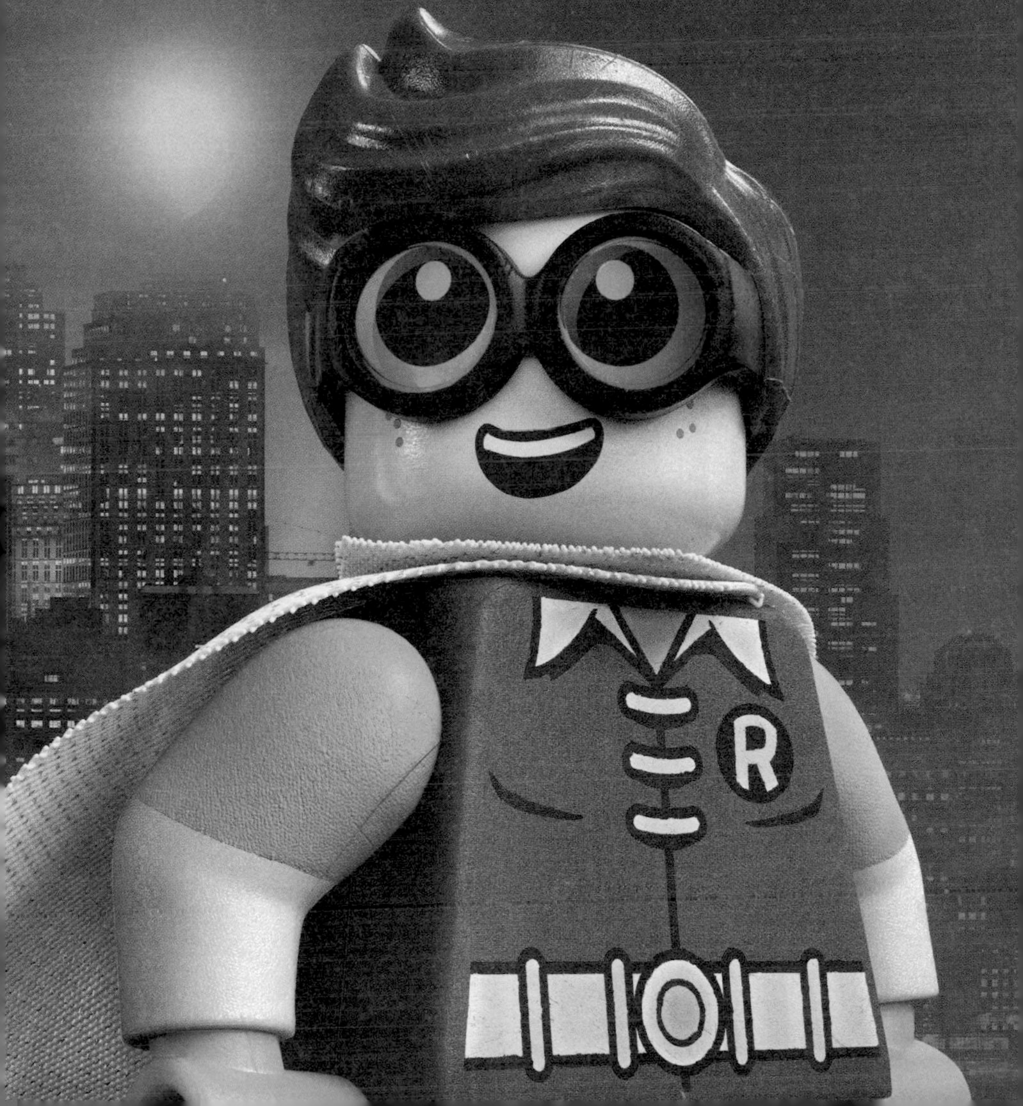
R

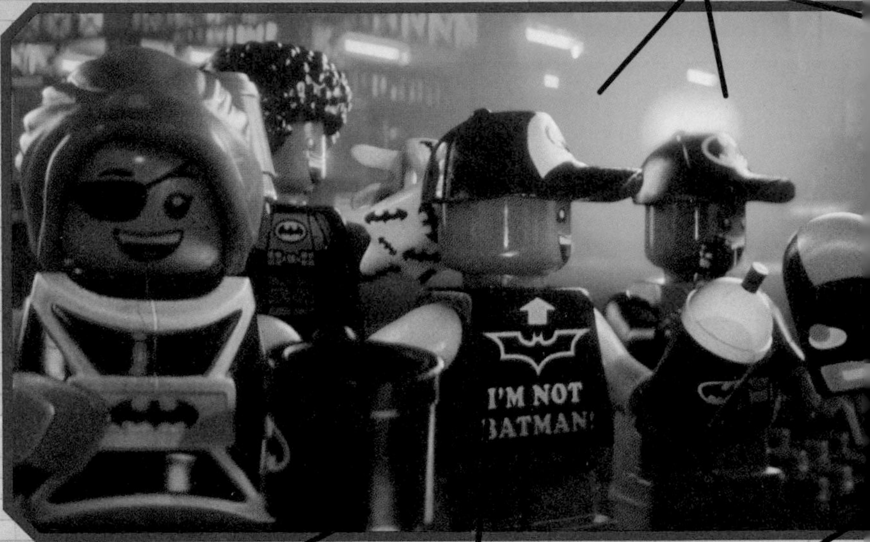
BATMAN CAPS
I'M NOT
BATMAN!
BATMAN
MUG
BATMAN T-SHIRT
BATMAN
LUNCH BOX

BATMAN MERCH

When I was at the orphanage, my dream was to be like Batman. That was the dream of all the other kids, too. (It was a popular dream.) We always wore our Batman merch to show our Caped Crusader pride!

BATMAN ICE CREAM

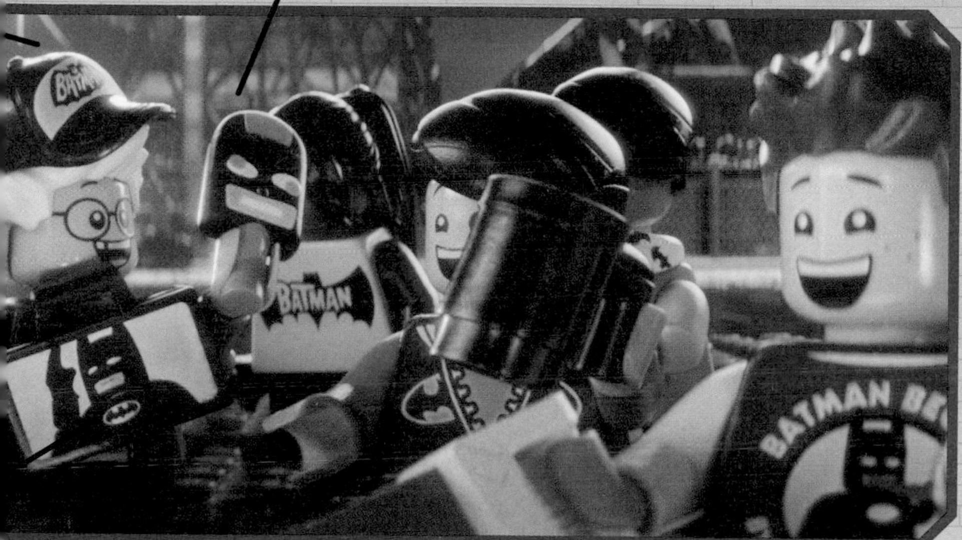
BATMAN
BATMAN BE

GROOVY GETUP

I never feel cool(er) than when I'm wearing my Robin costume. It's not because it's flashy or expensive. It's just so *me*.

And that's what dressing the part is all about! Whatever clothes make you feel special are the perfect match to your cool(er) self.

Collared shirts? Looking good!

Sweater vests? More like *bet*ter vests!

It's about finding a style that suits you, and then suiting up!

I FEEL LIKE I WAS POURED INTO THIS.

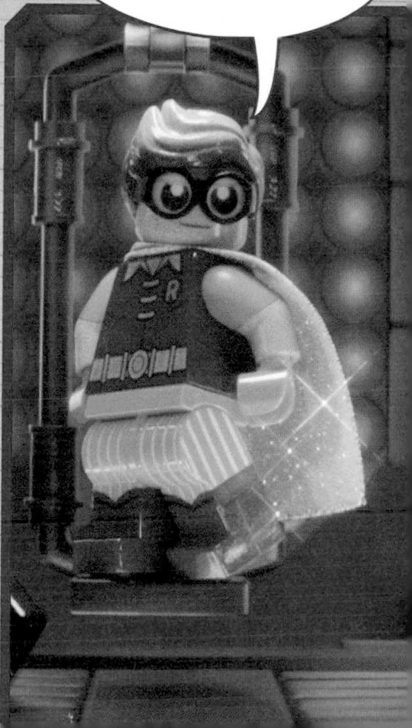

DRESS-UP PARTY

The Batcave has loads of cool costumes for me to try on. That's how I found the one that suits me just right. Check it out!

FLAMES: Feel the burn!

GLAM: It's all about that rockin' electric guitar!

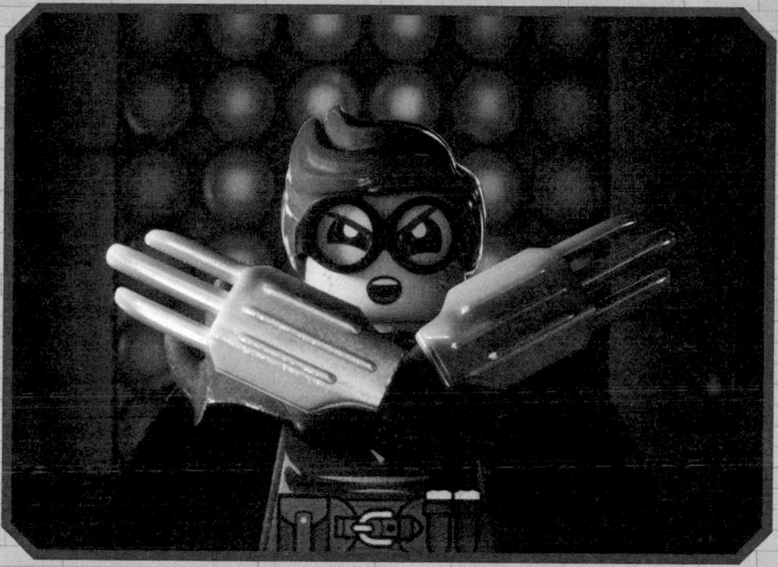

CLAWS: Looking sharp!

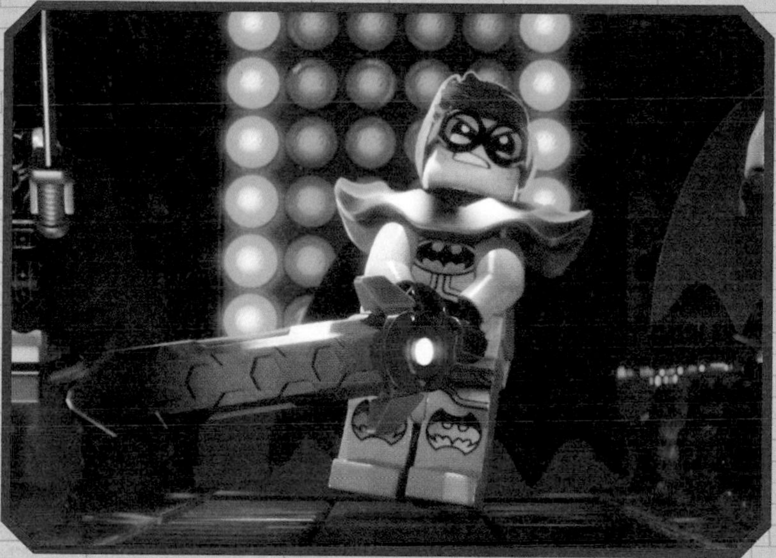

EX-CALI-BAT: Just call me a sidekick in shining armor!

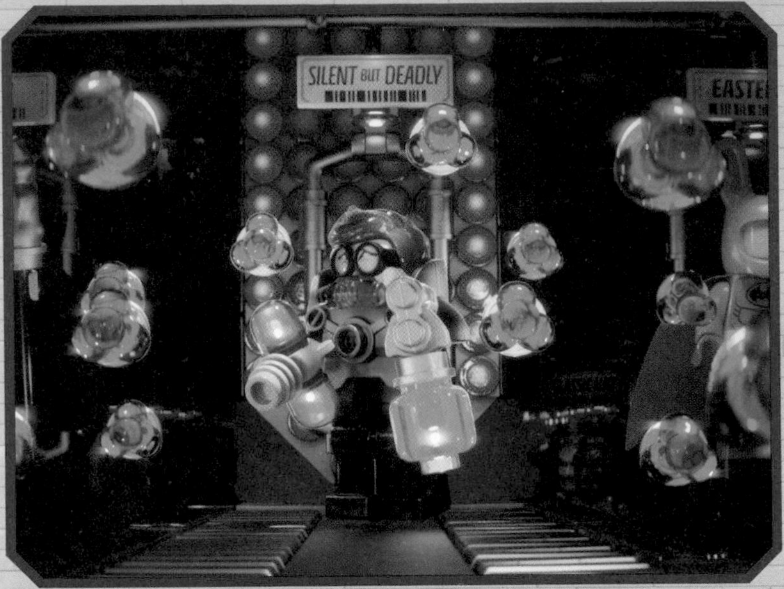
SILENT BUT DEADLY
EASTE

SILENT BUT DEADLY: Now that's one stylish toot suit.

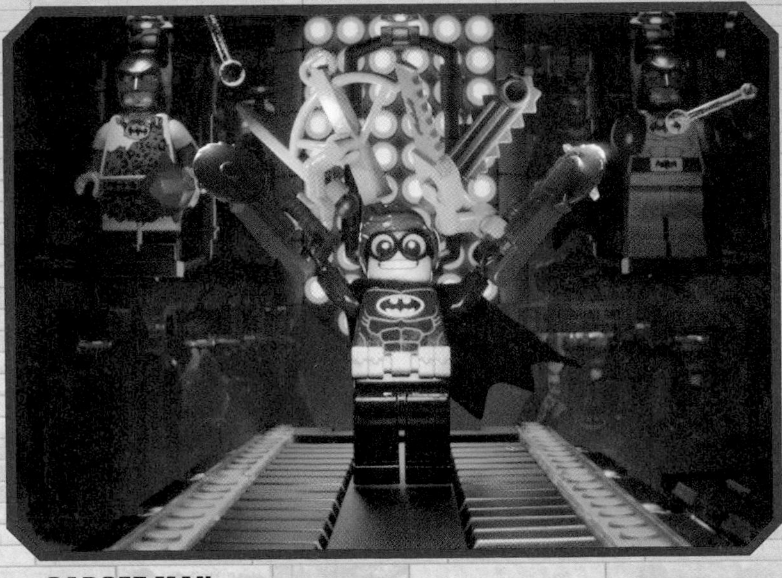

GADGET MAN: So many gadgets to choose from!

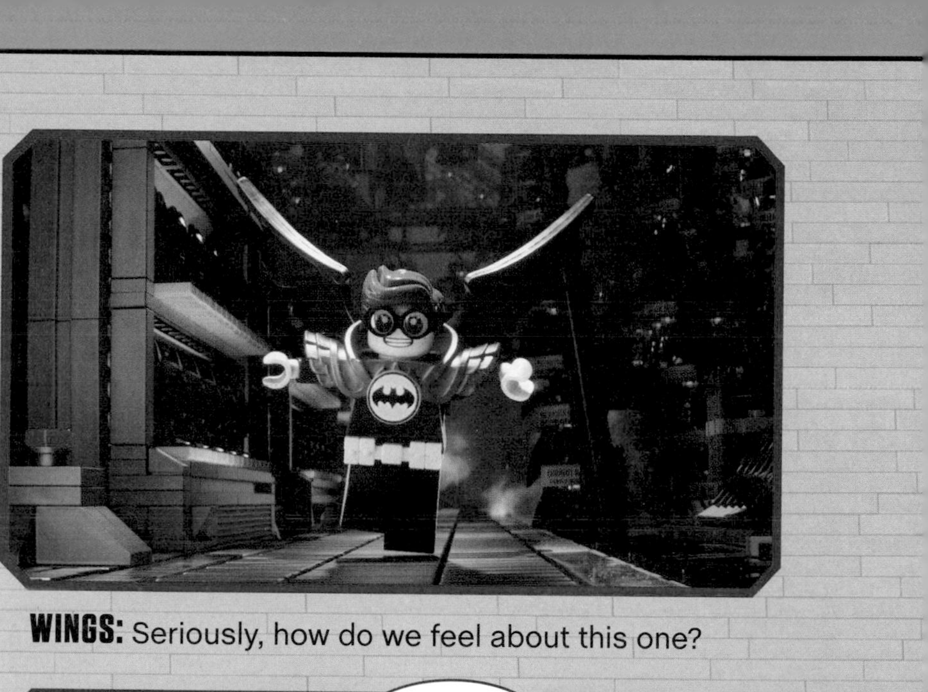

WINGS: Seriously, how do we feel about this one?

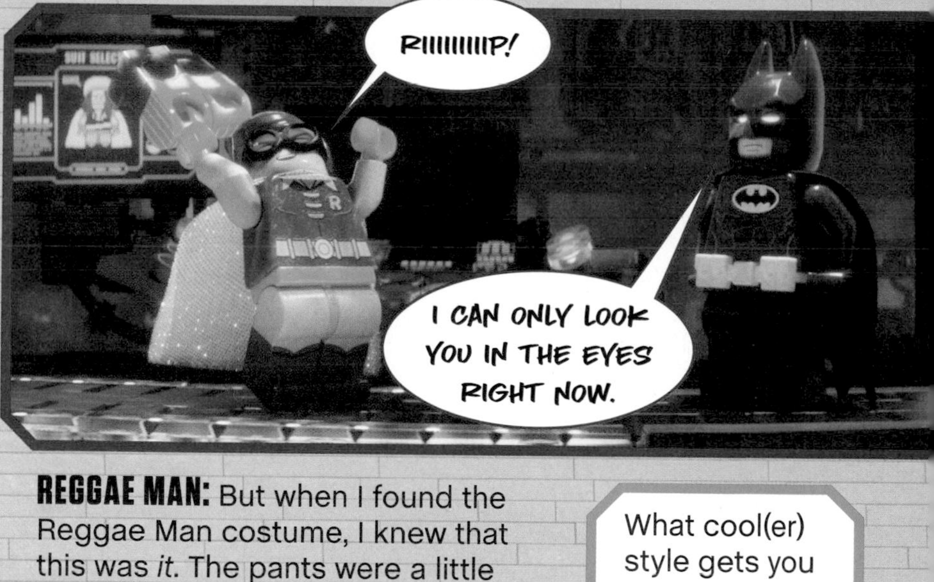
RIIIIIIIIP!
I CAN ONLY LOOK YOU IN THE EYES RIGHT NOW.

REGGAE MAN: But when I found the Reggae Man costume, I knew that this was *it*. The pants were a little tight. But with one big *riiiiip*, I was free and moving!

What cool(er) style gets you grooving?

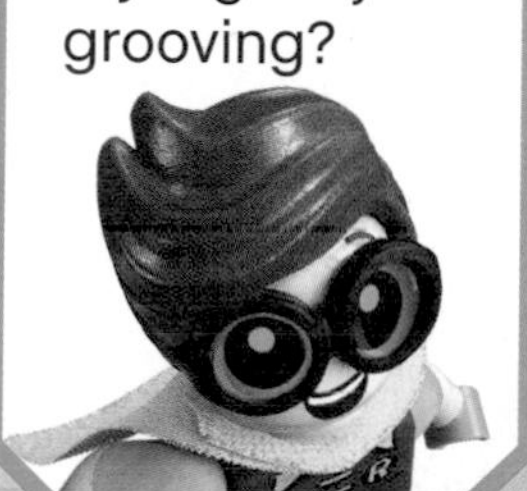

KICK YOUR STYLE UP A COOL(ER) NOTCH

Whatever your dream role, nothing beats that oh-so-fine feeling of looking *fine*. Here are my nifty tips for dressing the part.

1. **EXPLORER:** A compass and a telescope are all you need to get that set-sail vibe going.

2. **SCIENTIST:** It's a fact that people take you 99 percent more seriously if you wear glasses. 100 percent more if you break out the goggles. And extra style points for using the bottoms of soda bottles for lenses!

3. **ADVENTURER:** I hear eyeliner and eye patches are very fetching.

4. **SPORTS STAR:** Helmets and kneepads: good for sports practice *and* everyday safety.

5. **DOCTOR:** Clipboards are key. Doesn't matter what's on them. Just ABC: Always Be Clipboarding.

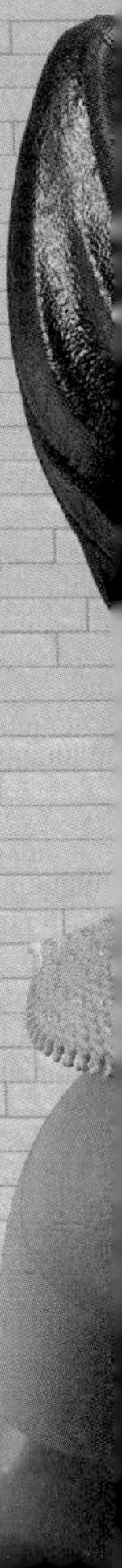

6. TEACHER: With a straitlaced sweater vest, you're sure to earn an A for style.

7. REPORTER: This just in: A cool hat and a notepad win the "first in news fashion" award.

8. LAWYER: No one will object to your legal prowess in a button-down shirt and tie.

9. COWBOY: Yee-haw! Saddle up with a kickin' pair of boots to bring out that inner wild, wild west.

10. SUPER HERO: Black. Like my old man says, the best Super Heroes always dress in black.

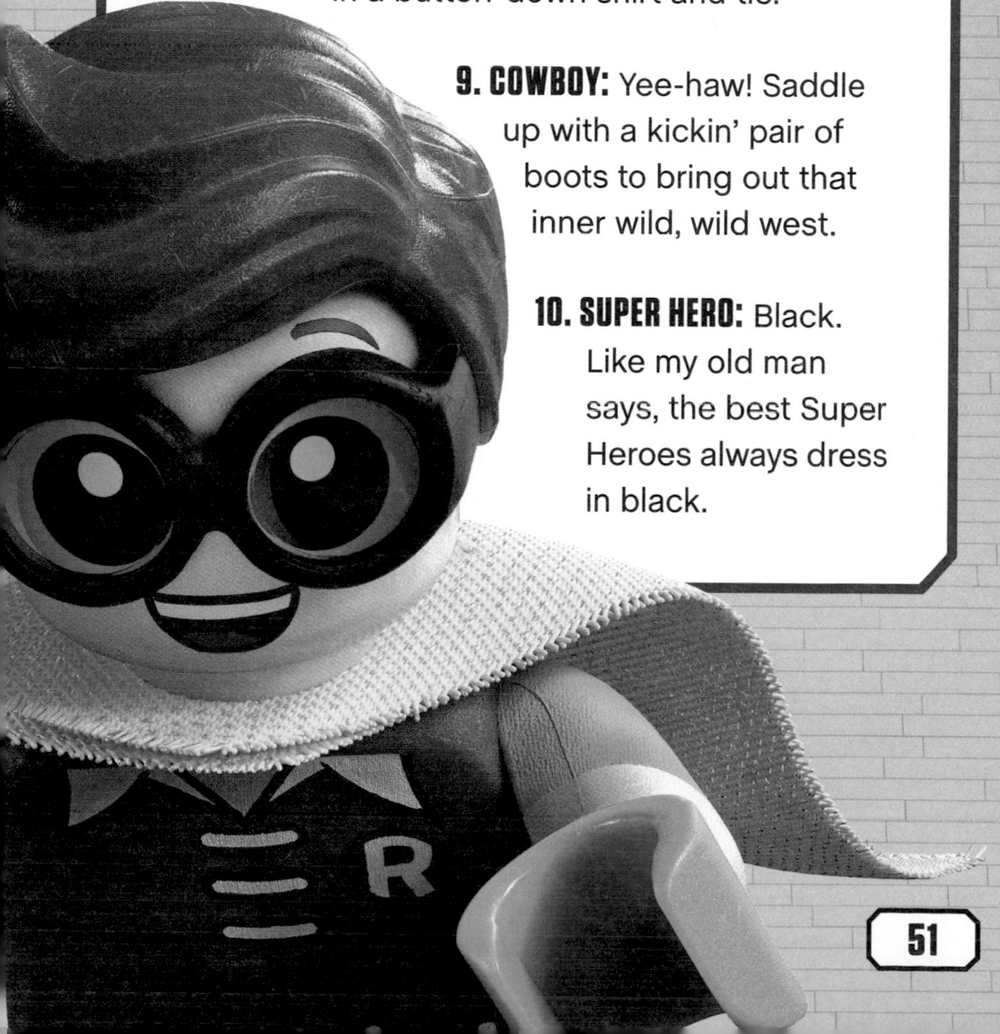

COOL(ER) LIFE LESSON #3:

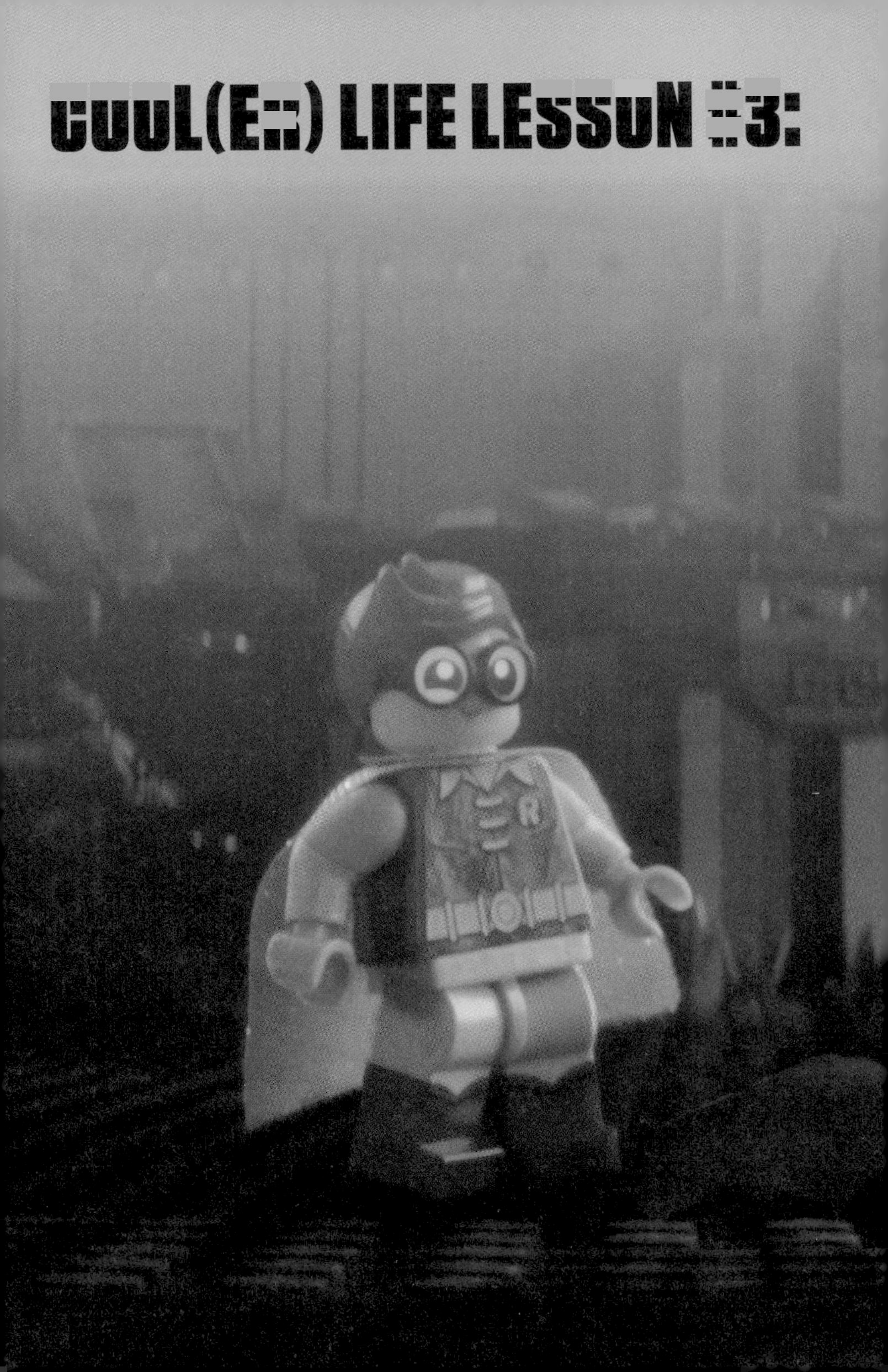

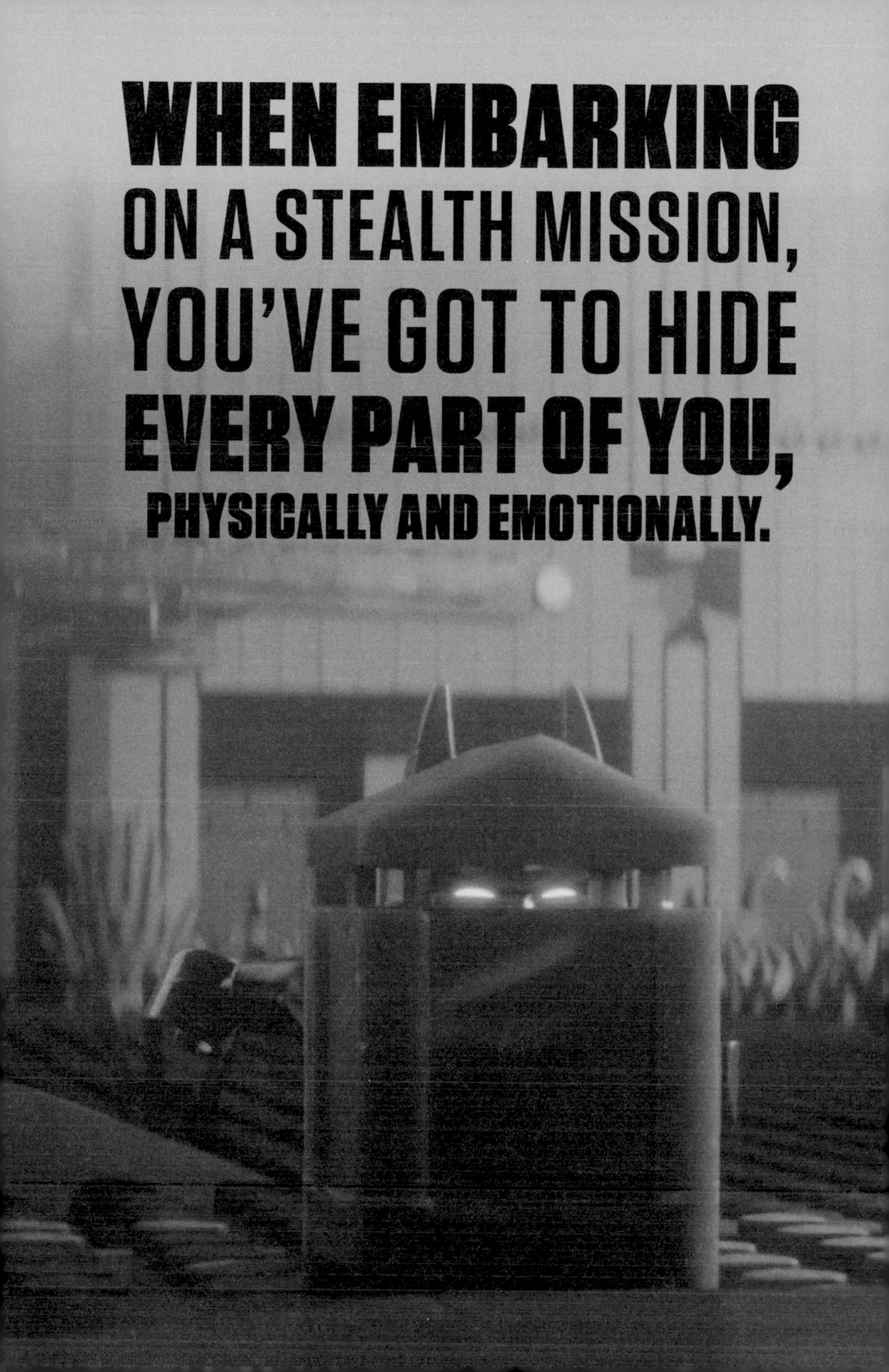
WHEN EMBARKING
ON A STEALTH MISSION,
YOU'VE GOT TO HIDE
EVERY PART OF YOU,
PHYSICALLY AND EMOTIONALLY.

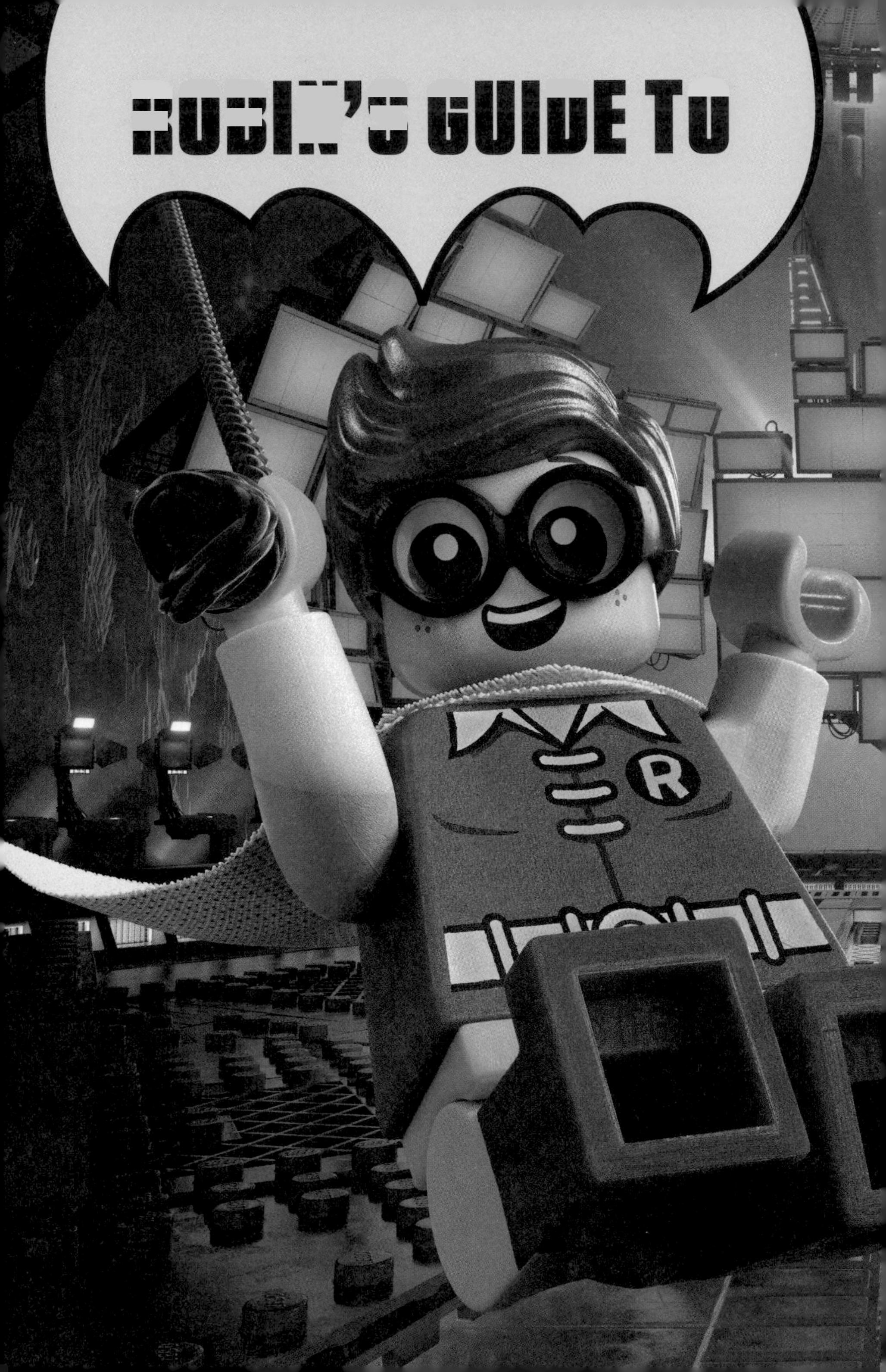
ROBIN'S GUIDE TO

GETTING GROOVY: GOING ON COOL(ER) MISSIONS

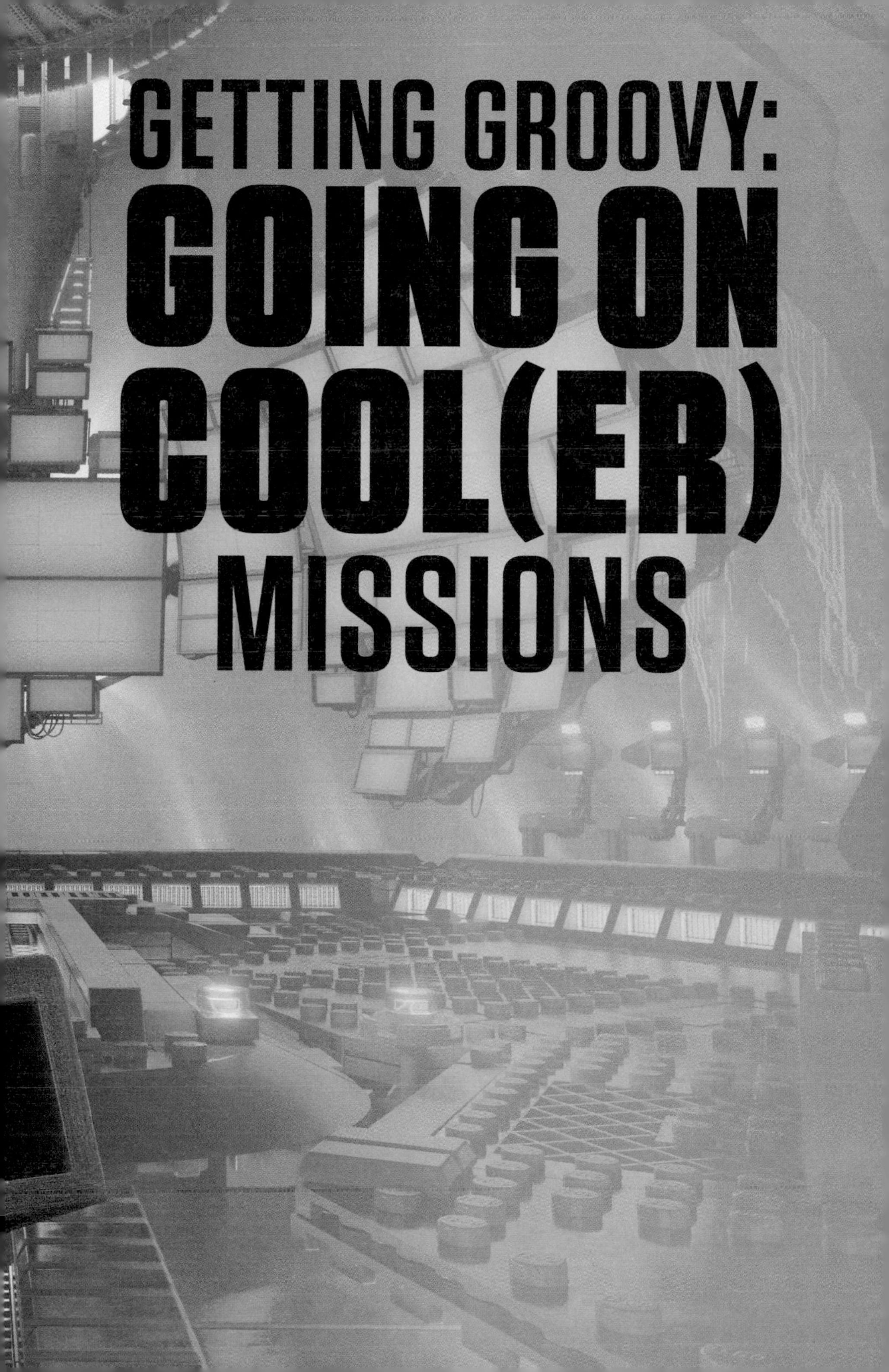

SUPER HERO MISSIONS = SUPER COOL!

Hot diggity dog, I just love going on super-secret stealth missions with Batman. He's always teaching me ways to be cool(er) whenever we're on the hunt to stop bad guys from a life of crime.

Check out these missions me and my papa went on to save Gotham City, and the lessons I learned along the way.

OPERATION: PHANTOM ZONE PROJECTOR

Batman needed the Phantom Zone Projector to zap the Joker to a dimension where he couldn't cause mischief anymore. Unfortunately, the projector was well guarded in Superman's Fortress of Solitude. By lasers. And fire. And an acid moat.

PHANTOM ZONE PROJECTOR
AUDIO OUT
PROJECTION
PZP-ANALYSIS FILE

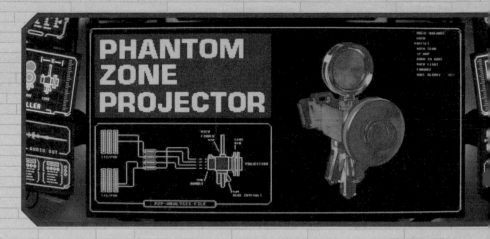

That's where I came in! Only someone nimble, quick, and quiet could sneak in and nab that projector. And I can be all three! (When I desire to be.)

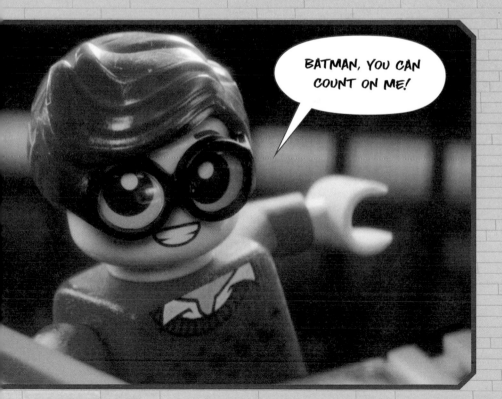

BATMAN, YOU CAN COUNT ON ME!

TOES TO THE NOSE

The only way for me to reach the Phantom Zone Projector was to follow Batman's instructions *exactly.* So that's what I did! I flipped. I kicked. I freestyled. And I nabbed that projector faster than you can say "Zap it to me!"

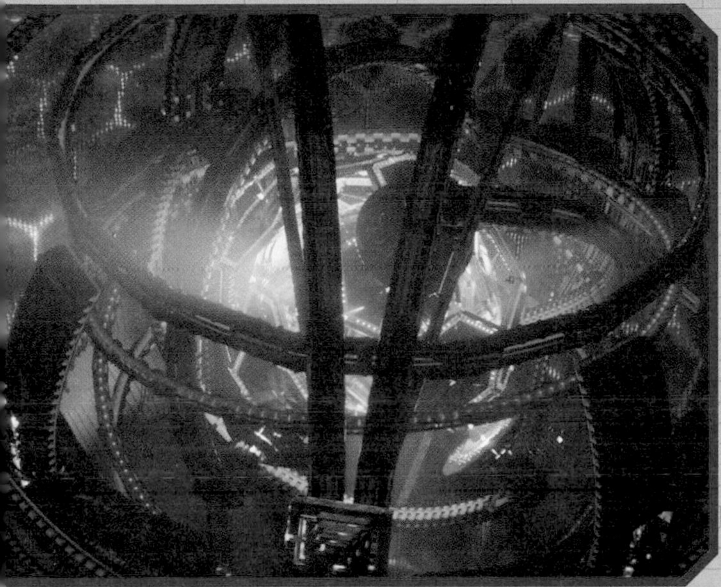

I was so happy to be working with Batman as a team. And get this—Batman was proud of me, too! My papa was proud of me! And if you ask me, that's as cool(er) as it gets.

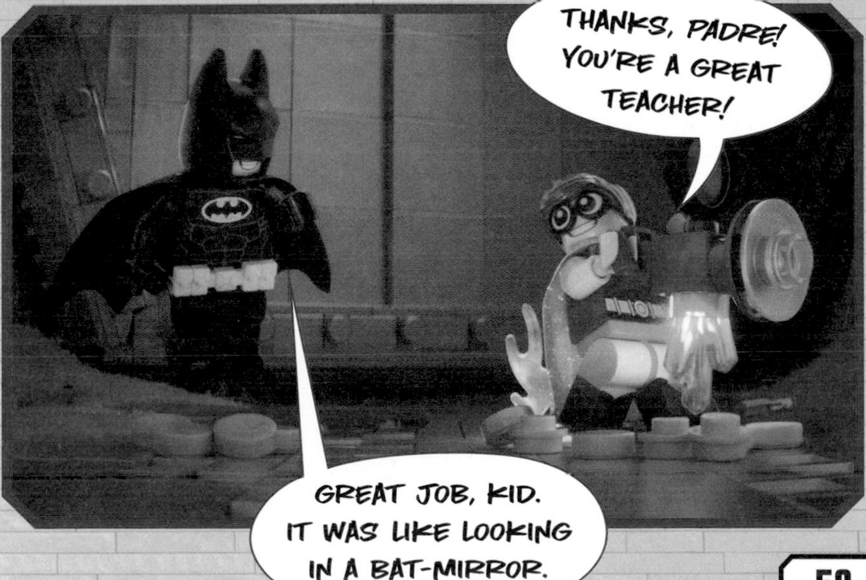
THANKS, PADRE! YOU'RE A GREAT TEACHER!
GREAT JOB, KID. IT WAS LIKE LOOKING IN A BAT-MIRROR.

OPERATION: JAIL BREAK

I'm not quite sure why, but once my Bat-dad used the Phantom Zone Projector to send the Joker to the Phantom Zone, the new police commissioner, Barbara Gordon, was pretty darn mad. She even locked us up in jail! But I didn't mind. As long as I was doing a dime in the big house with my old man, I knew things would be A-OK.

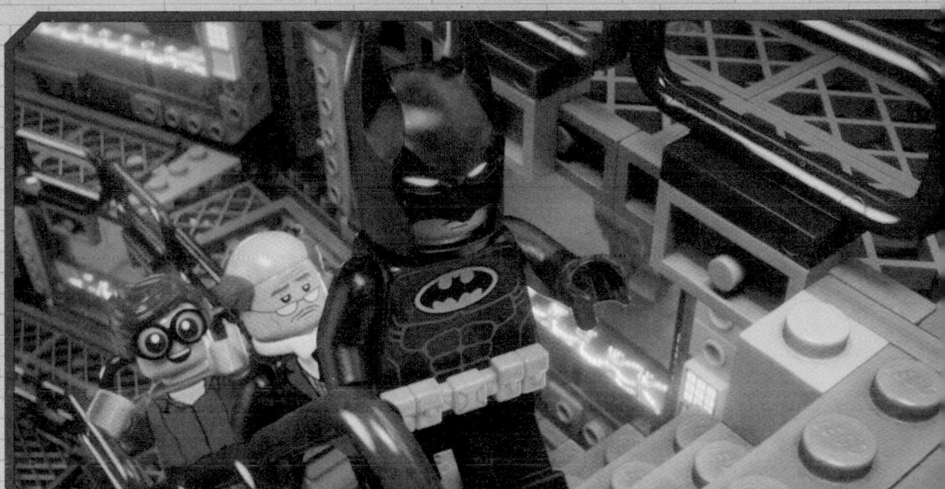

As it turned out, the Joker escaped from the Phantom Zone with a lot of mega-bad guys. So Barbara Gordon let us out to help her stop them! Alfred came, too. It was a family trip to save the city—cool!

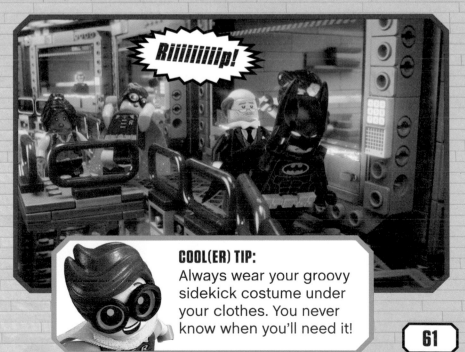

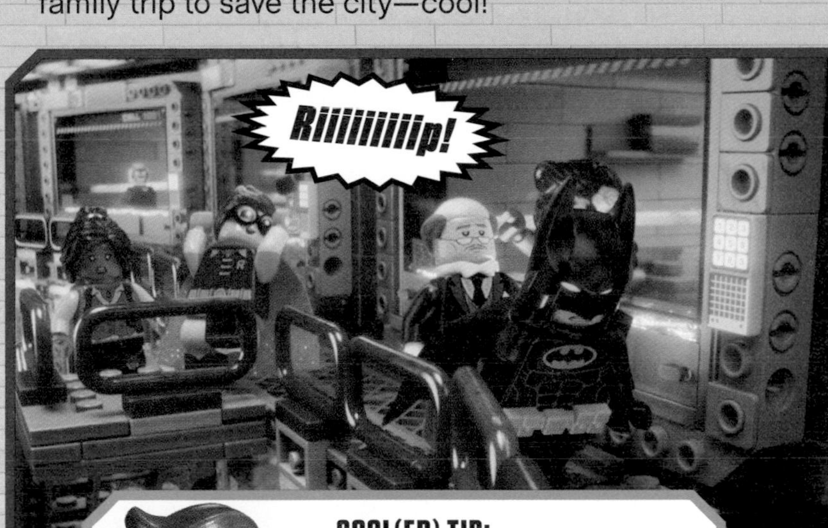
Riiiiiiiiip!

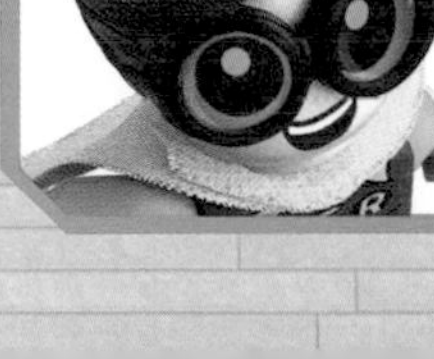

COOL(ER) TIP:
Always wear your groovy sidekick costume under your clothes. You never know when you'll need it!

OPERATION: SAVE THE CITY!

This is the Joker. He and Batman have a . . . complicated relationship. The Joker can be pretty bad to the bone. But he also wants to make Batman proud of his evil escapades. So I guess he's kind of like me, in a bad-guy way.

Together with the bad guys from the Phantom Zone, the Joker took over Gotham City. He even turned my Bat-dad's Wayne Island into the Joker Island. That was *not* cool(er)!

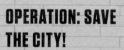

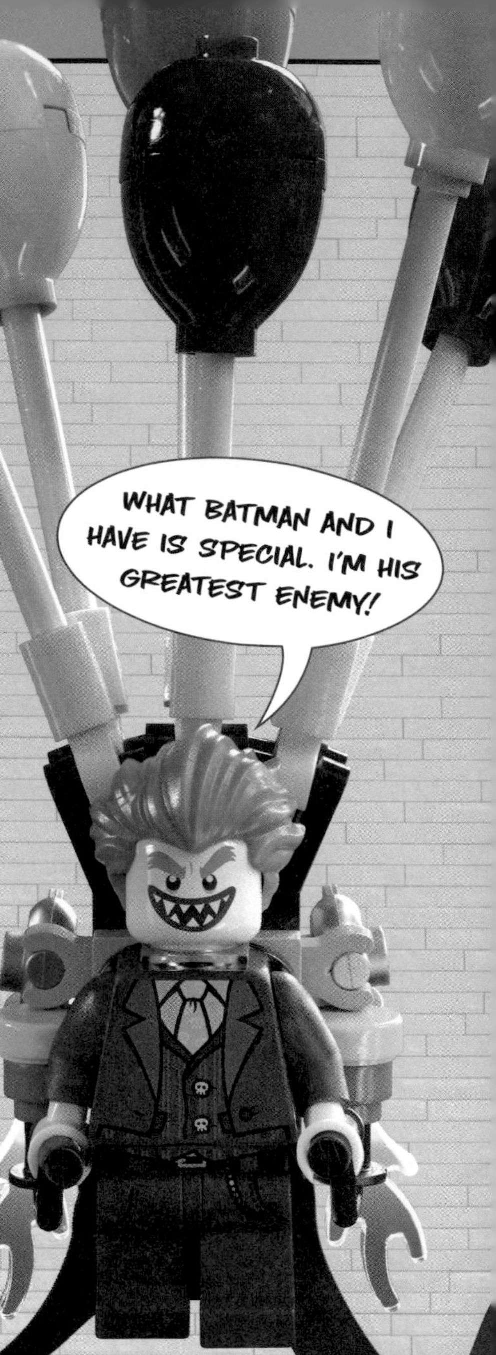

WHAT BATMAN AND I HAVE IS SPECIAL. I'M HIS GREATEST ENEMY!

It was up to me, my dad, Alfred, and Barbara Gordon to stop him. And if there's one überimportant thing I learned during this whole wild and crazy ride, it's that you have to work with your cool(er) team to get the job done.

COOL(ER)

NOT COOL(ER)!

OPERATION: SAVE THE CITY!

Working together, we showed those bad guys who was boss. We sent them all back to the Phantom Zone, but not before a bomb went off and split the city in two. Gotham City was collapsing!

But then, the ultimate cool(er) moment happened. Batman convinced the Joker that without Gotham City, there would be no Batman and Joker. And the Joker didn't want that! So we all worked together to pull the city back together—literally. Woo-hoo! Gotham was saved!

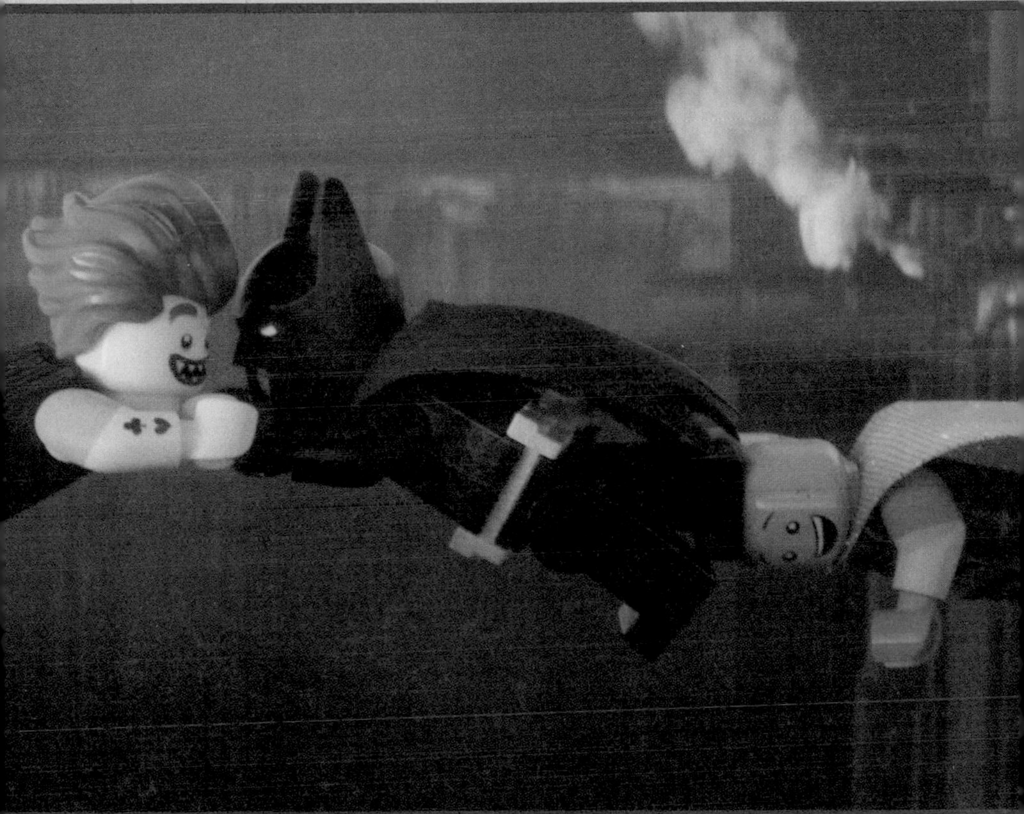

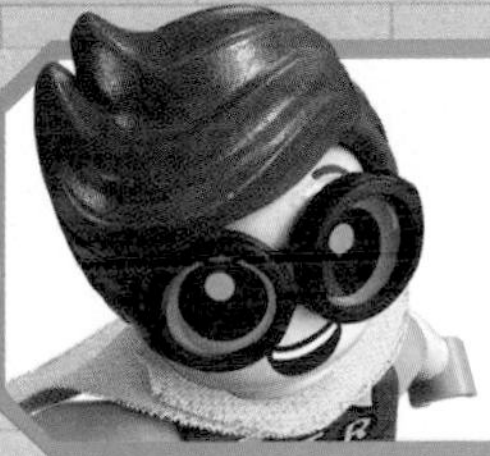

COOL(ER) TIP:
Shredded abs are super helpful when saving the city.

OPERATION: FAMILY TIES

After all those missions, I was feeling pretty jazzed. Had I made my Daddy-o proud? Check! Had we beatboxed our way out of the clink? You betcha! Had we saved Gotham City from imminent destruction using nothing but sheer determination and sick core strength? Heck yeah!

But the best thing by far was that I got to share all those missions with my new family. That's pretty much the coolest thing I can teach you: There's NOTHING cool(er) than family.

You see, all I ever wanted was a family of my own. And that's exactly what Batman wanted, too. So in a way, becoming a family was the greatest mission of all.

Of course, there were some growing pains along the way . . .

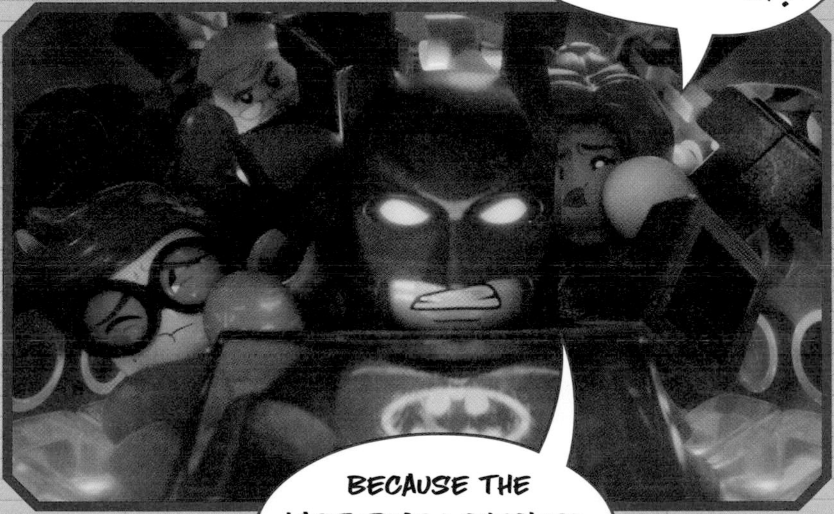
BATMAN, WHY DID YOU MAKE THIS THING WITH ONLY ONE SEAT?
BECAUSE THE LAST TIME I CHECKED, I ONLY HAD ONE BUTT.

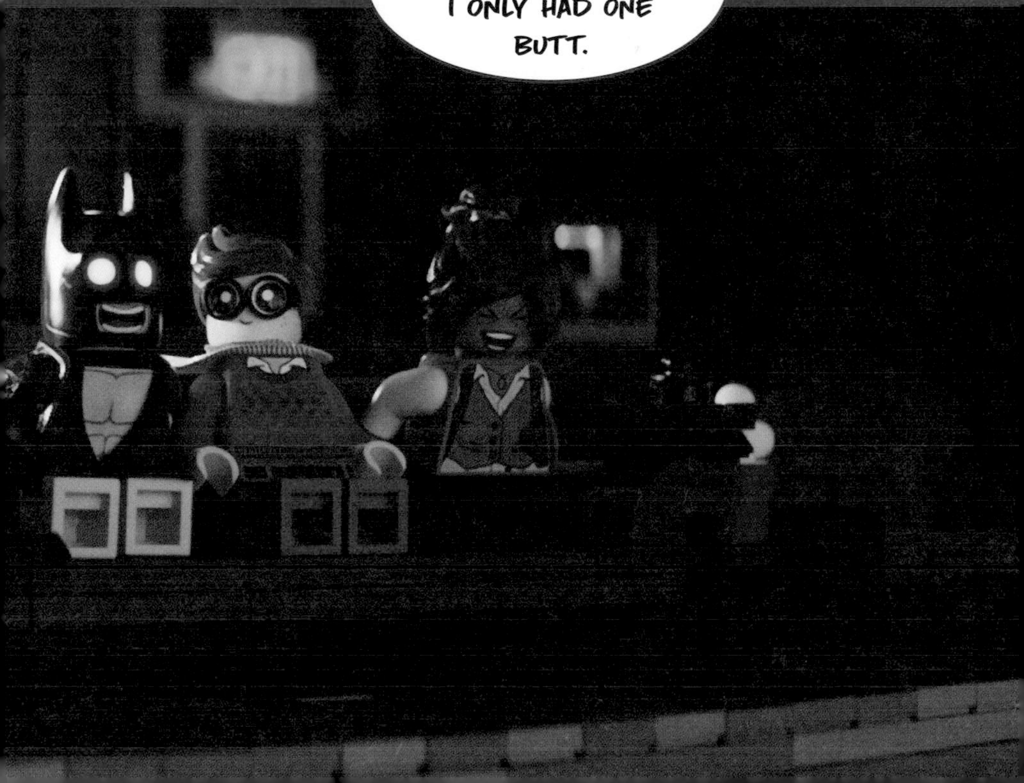

COOL(ER) LIFE LESSON #4:

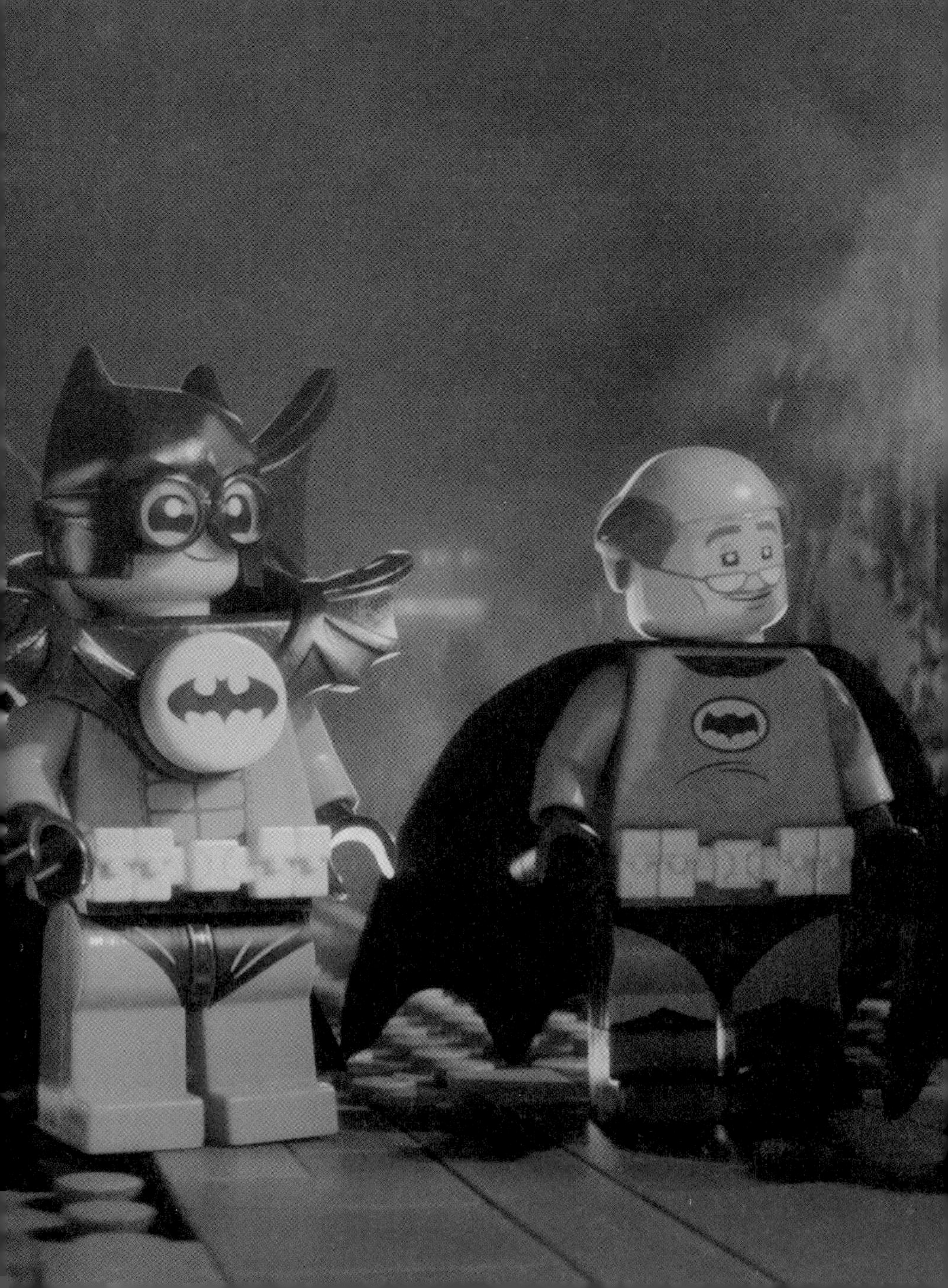

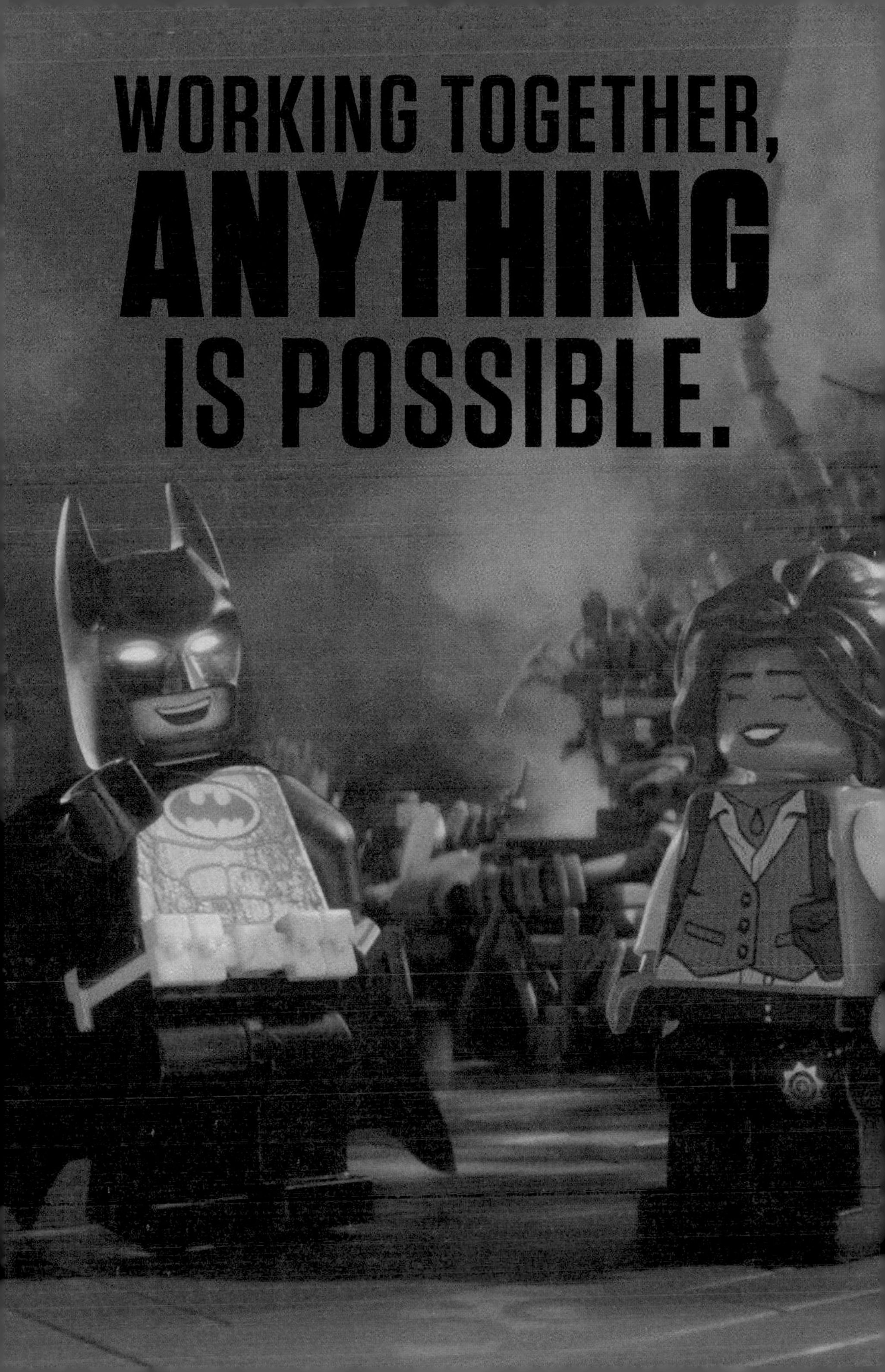
WORKING TOGETHER,
ANYTHING
IS POSSIBLE.

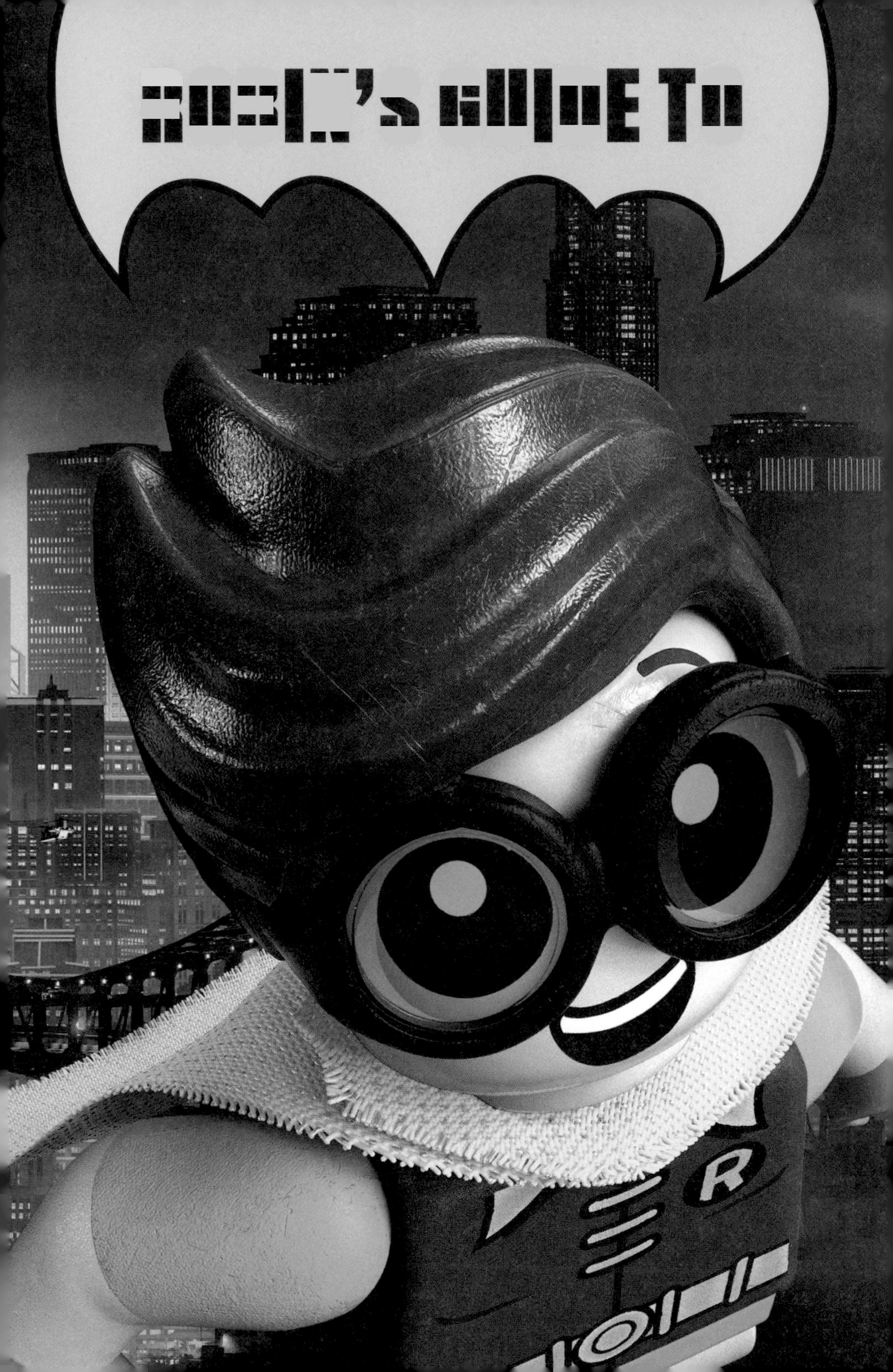
ROBIN'S GUIDE TO

SPEAKING THE LINGO

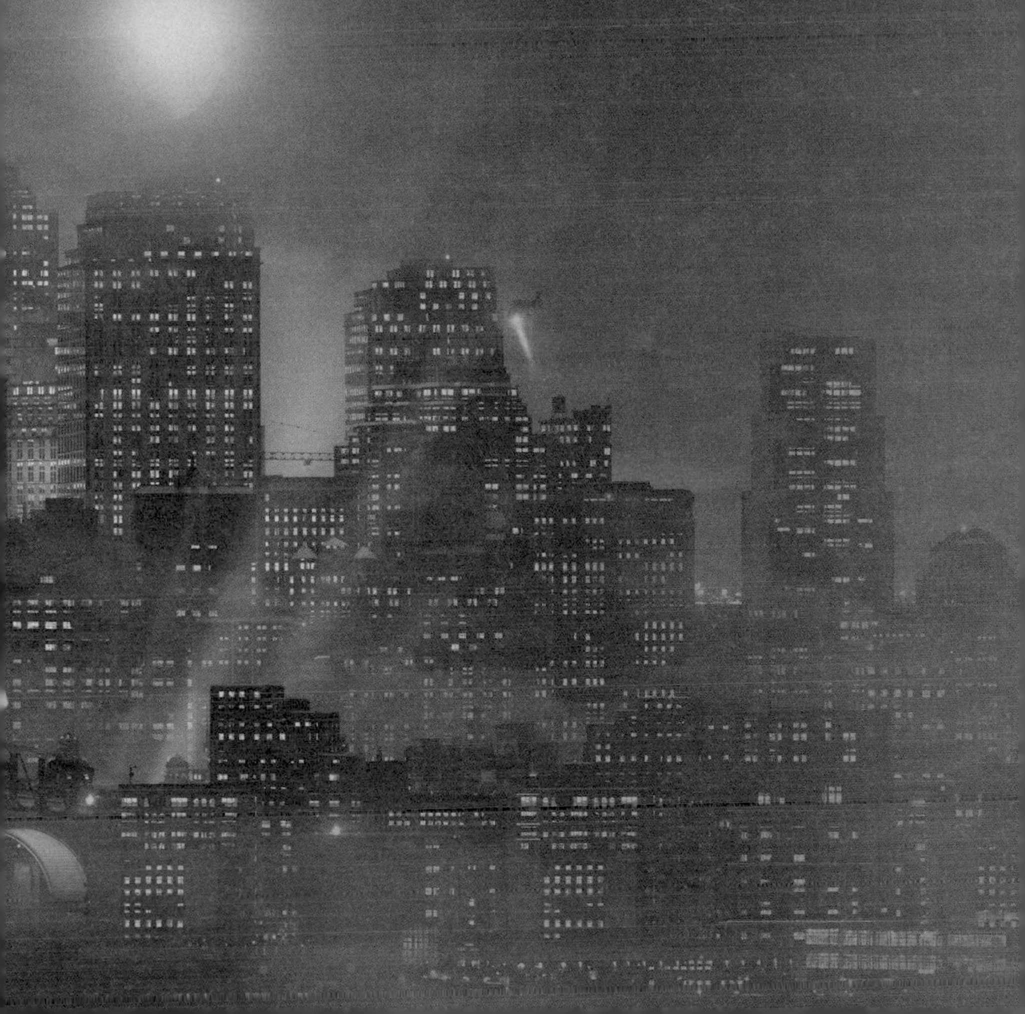

GOOD CATCHPHRASES

So you've learned to walk the cool(er) walk. But can you talk the cool(er) talk?

When you're in the business of kicking criminal tushies and taking names, you need a few catchy catchphrases along the way. Here are some of my favorites.

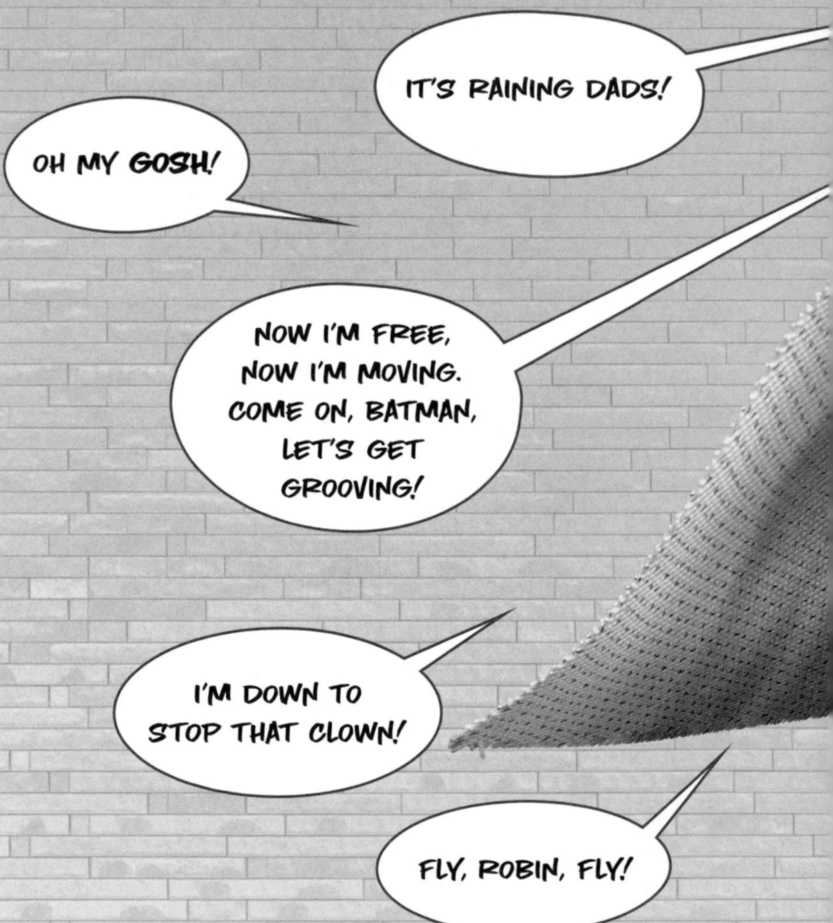
IT'S RAINING DADS!
OH MY GOSH!
NOW I'M FREE, NOW I'M MOVING. COME ON, BATMAN, LET'S GET GROOVING!
I'M DOWN TO STOP THAT CLOWN!
FLY, ROBIN, FLY!

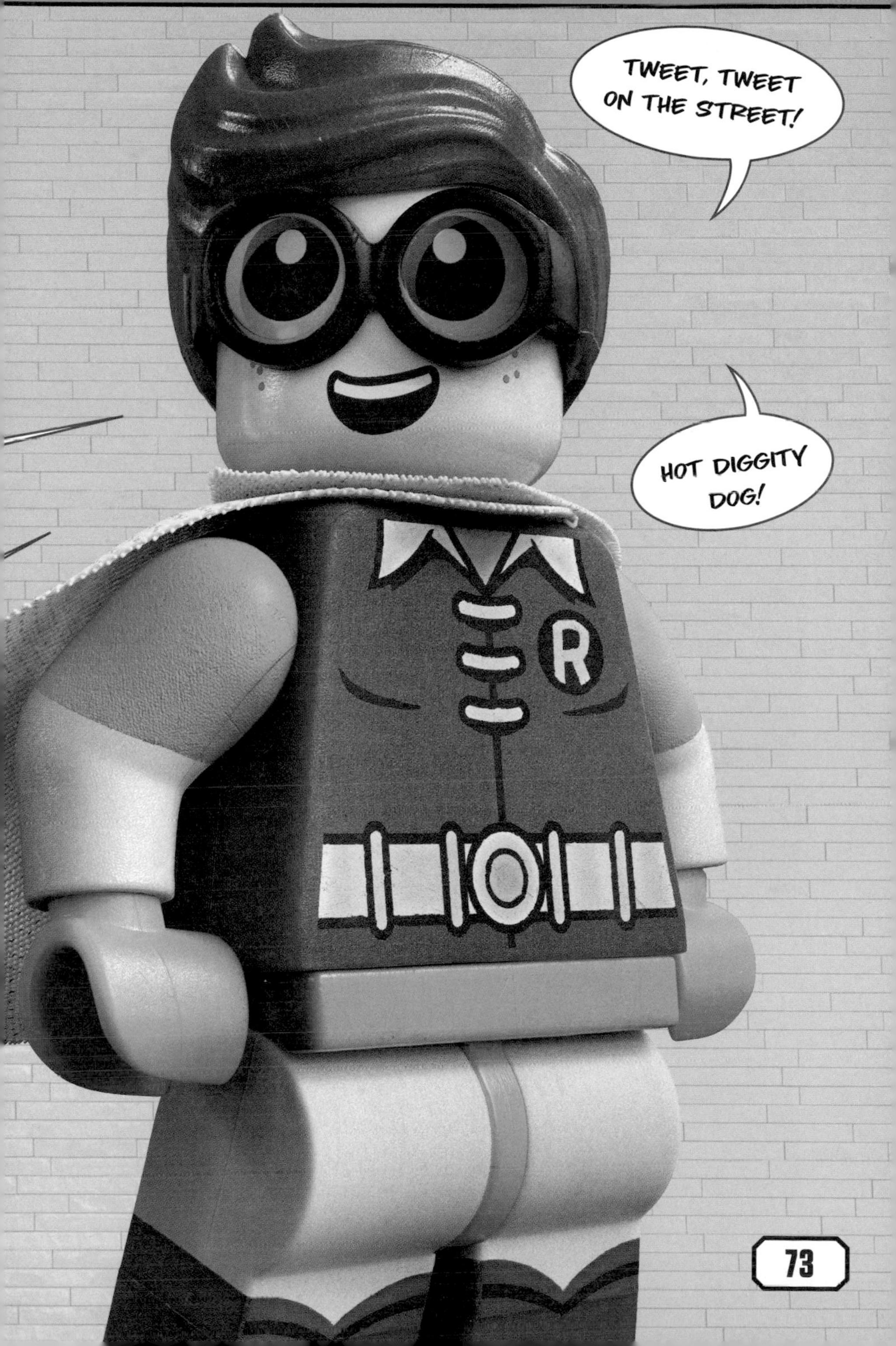
TWEET, TWEET ON THE STREET!
HOT DIGGITY DOG!

FAILED CATCHPHRASES

For every good catchphrase, there are going to be a few clunkers. But did I let a few silly slipups get me down? Gosh, no! I just always make sure to ask my dad for his thoughts on my latest slogan du jour.

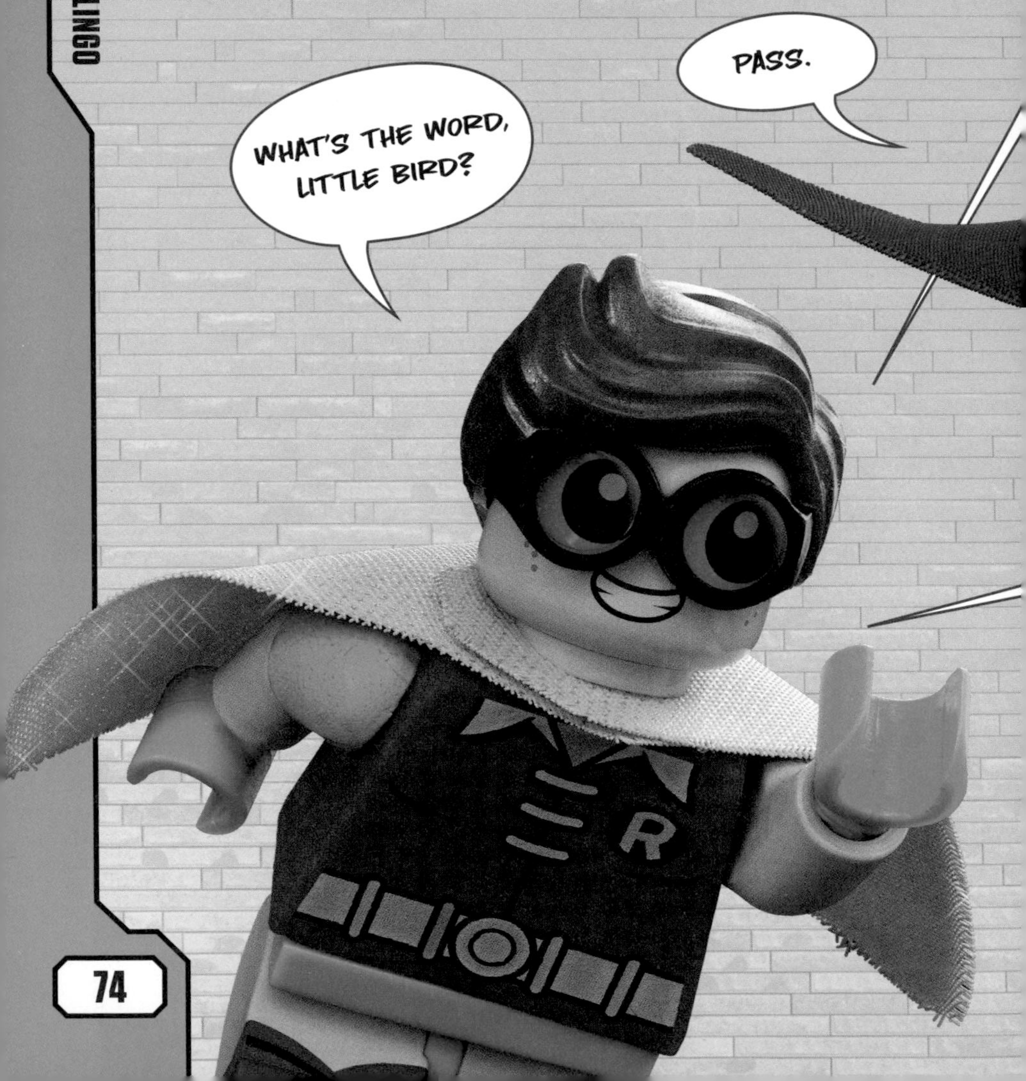
WHAT'S THE WORD, LITTLE BIRD?
PASS.

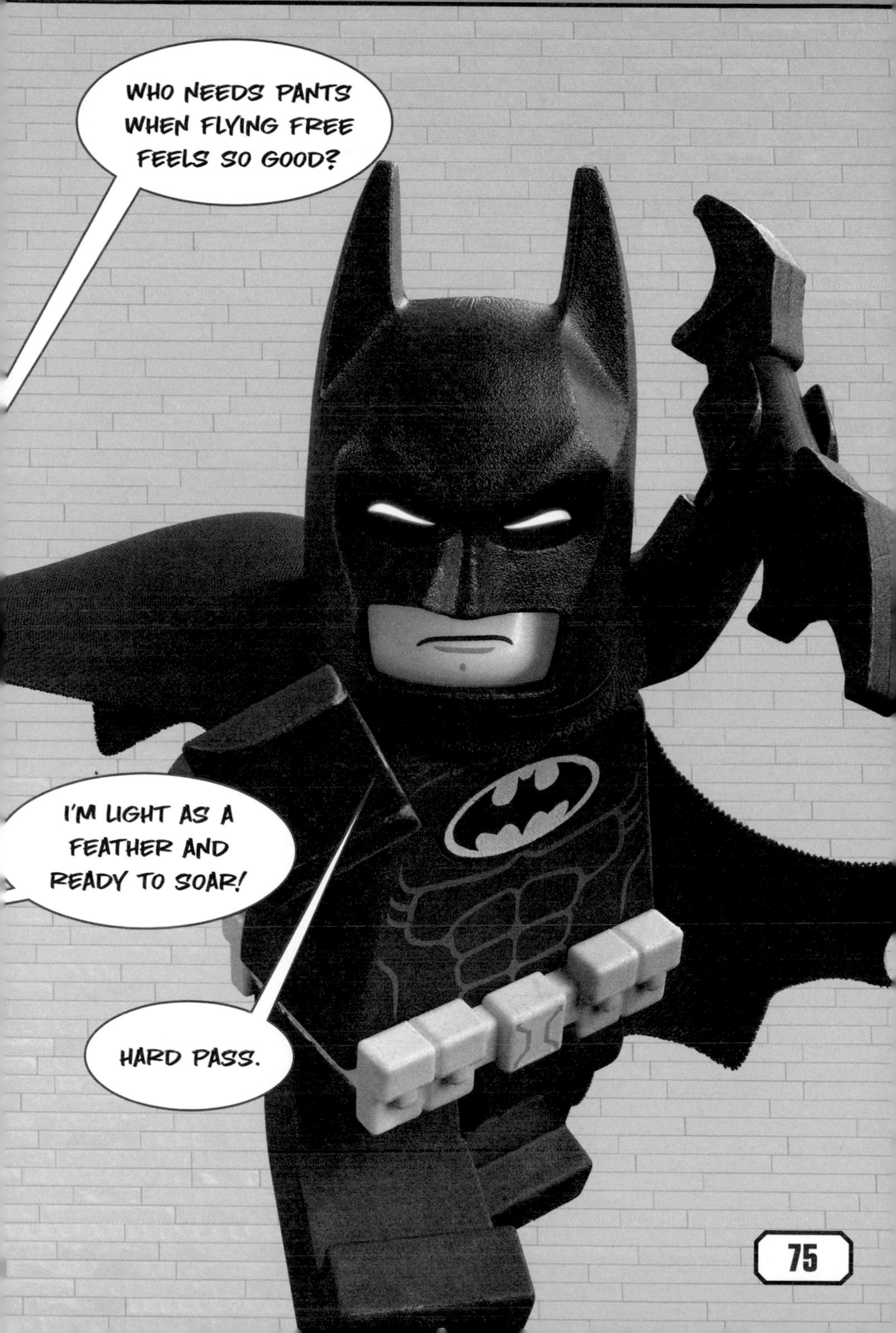
WHO NEEDS PANTS WHEN FLYING FREE FEELS SO GOOD?
I'M LIGHT AS A FEATHER AND READY TO SOAR!
HARD PASS.

SECURITY CAM 023
AUTO TRACKING [ON] OFF

FD 35.2987
59mm
10:48:29 AM
TCR 00:21:11:18   PLAY

CODE NAMES

Everyone knows that one of the most awesome things about being a Super Hero is having a sweet code name. How else can you communicate with your Super Hero *compadres* without anyone knowing your real identity? At the orphanage, I was always coming up with jazzy code names in case my dream of becoming Batman's sidekick ever came true.

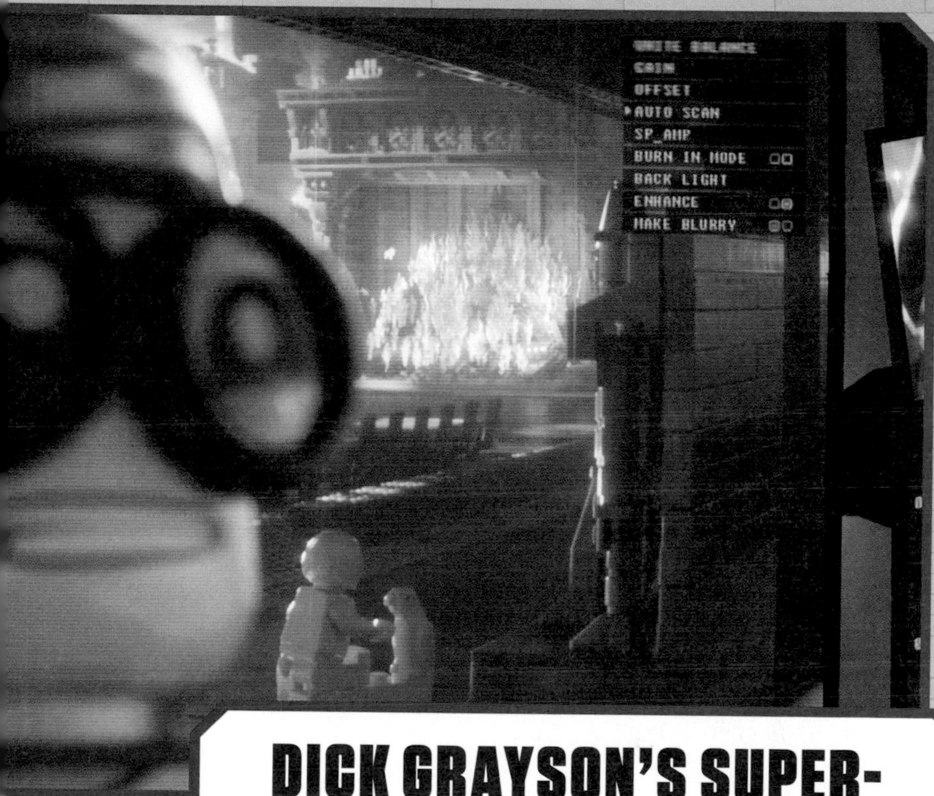
OFFSET
AUTO SCAN
SP_AMP
BURN IN MODE
BACK LIGHT
ENHANCE
MAKE BLURRY

DICK GRAYSON'S SUPER-SECRET CODE NAME LIST:

- Swan Boy
- Marvelous Meerkat
- Ultra Mouse
- Gymkata Kid
- Lemur Lad
- The Flying Squirrel

AND THE WINNER IS . . .

Robin! (clearly)

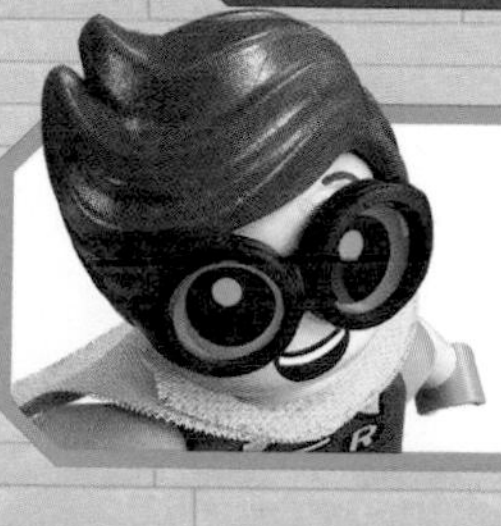

What's your secret code name?

MI PADRE ES BATMAN

Speaking of code names, sometimes you need other nickname options for your Super Hero dad. So it's helpful to have a few backup names to call your *padre* to make him feel special.

- Papa
- *Padre* (also a cool Spanish way to say "buddy")
- Bat-dad
- My old man
- Daddy-o #1 / Daddy-o #2
- *Otōsan*
- Pops
- Parental guardian

I DON'T ALWAYS DO "PARENTING." BUT WHEN I DO, I'M AN A+ *NUMERO UNO* SUPER HERO DAD.

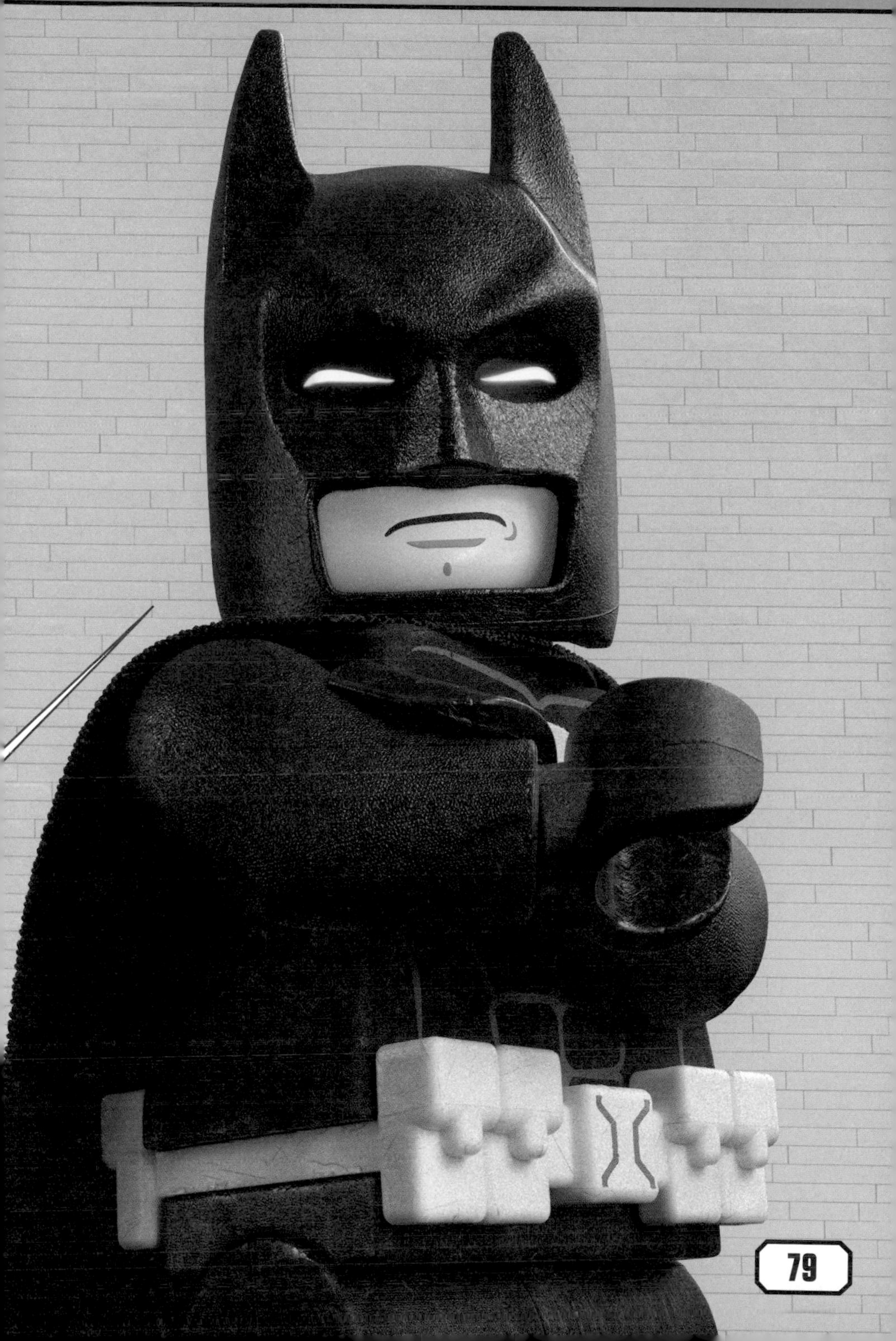

CATCHPHRASE GENERATOR

All right, fellow curtailers of crime! Are you ready to kick your sidekick game into high gear? It's time to come up with your own signature catchphrase! Choose one word from each column and discover your personal super slogan.

Always	Fly	Crazy
Go	Dance	Bananas
Don't	Look	Silly
Let's	Get	Nuts
Stop!	Fight	Groovy

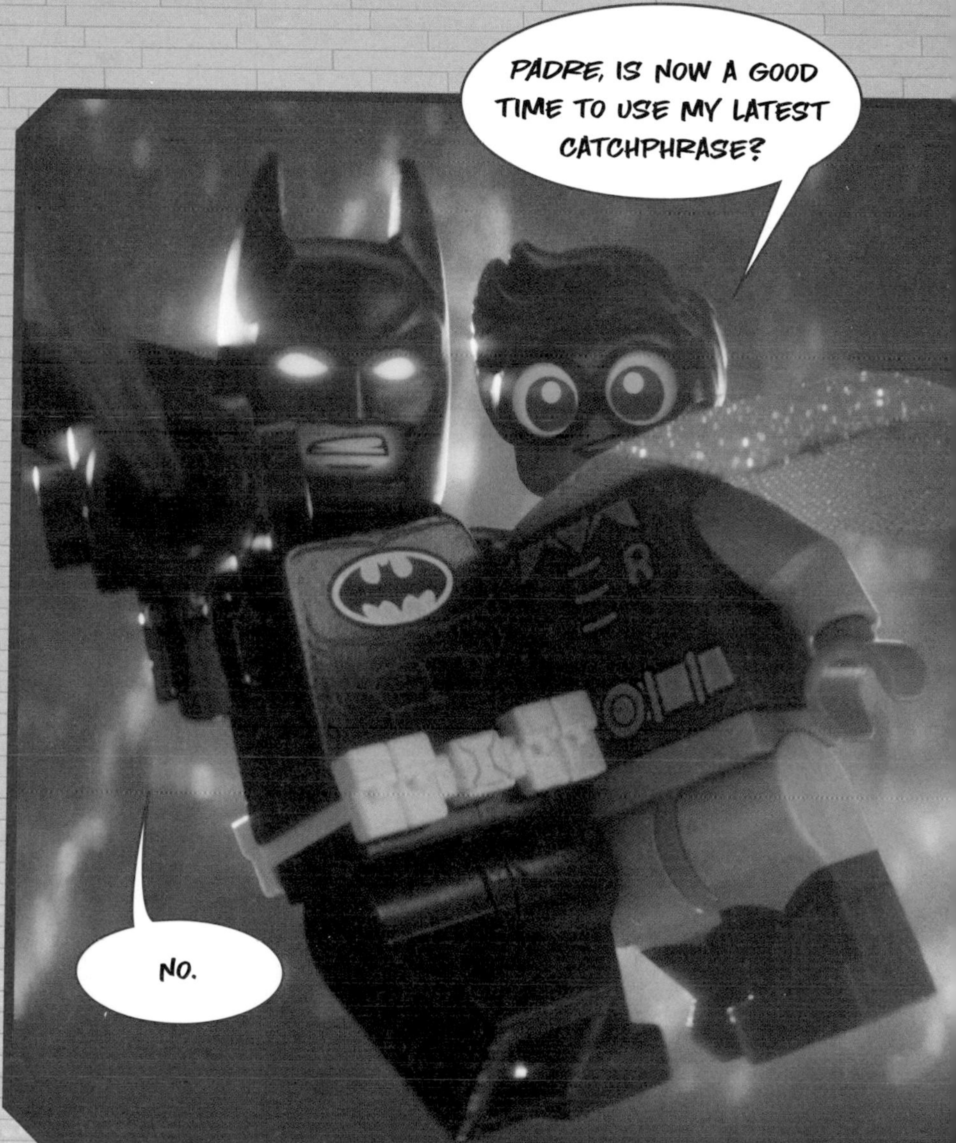
PADRE, IS NOW A GOOD TIME TO USE MY LATEST CATCHPHRASE?
NO.

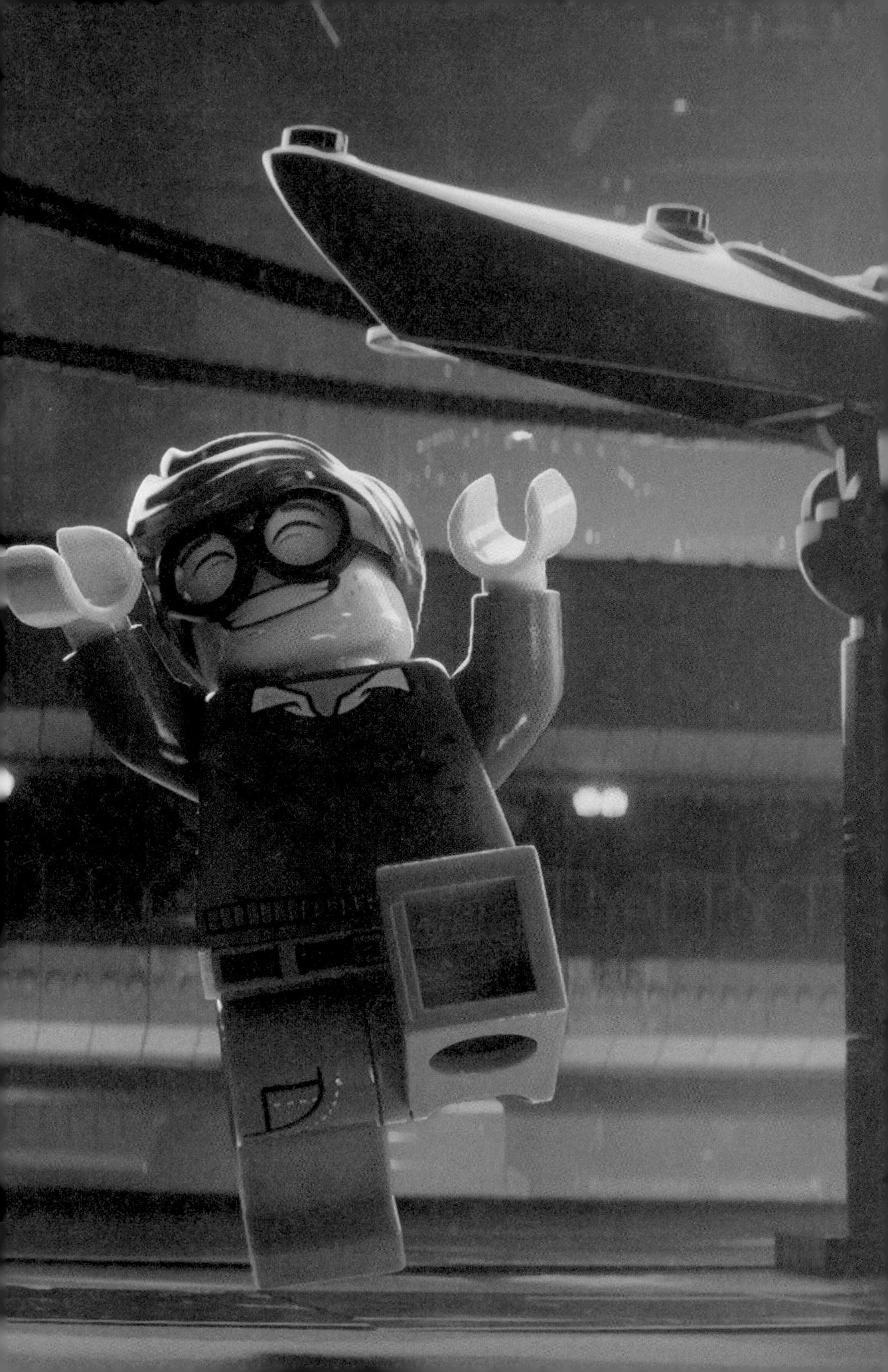

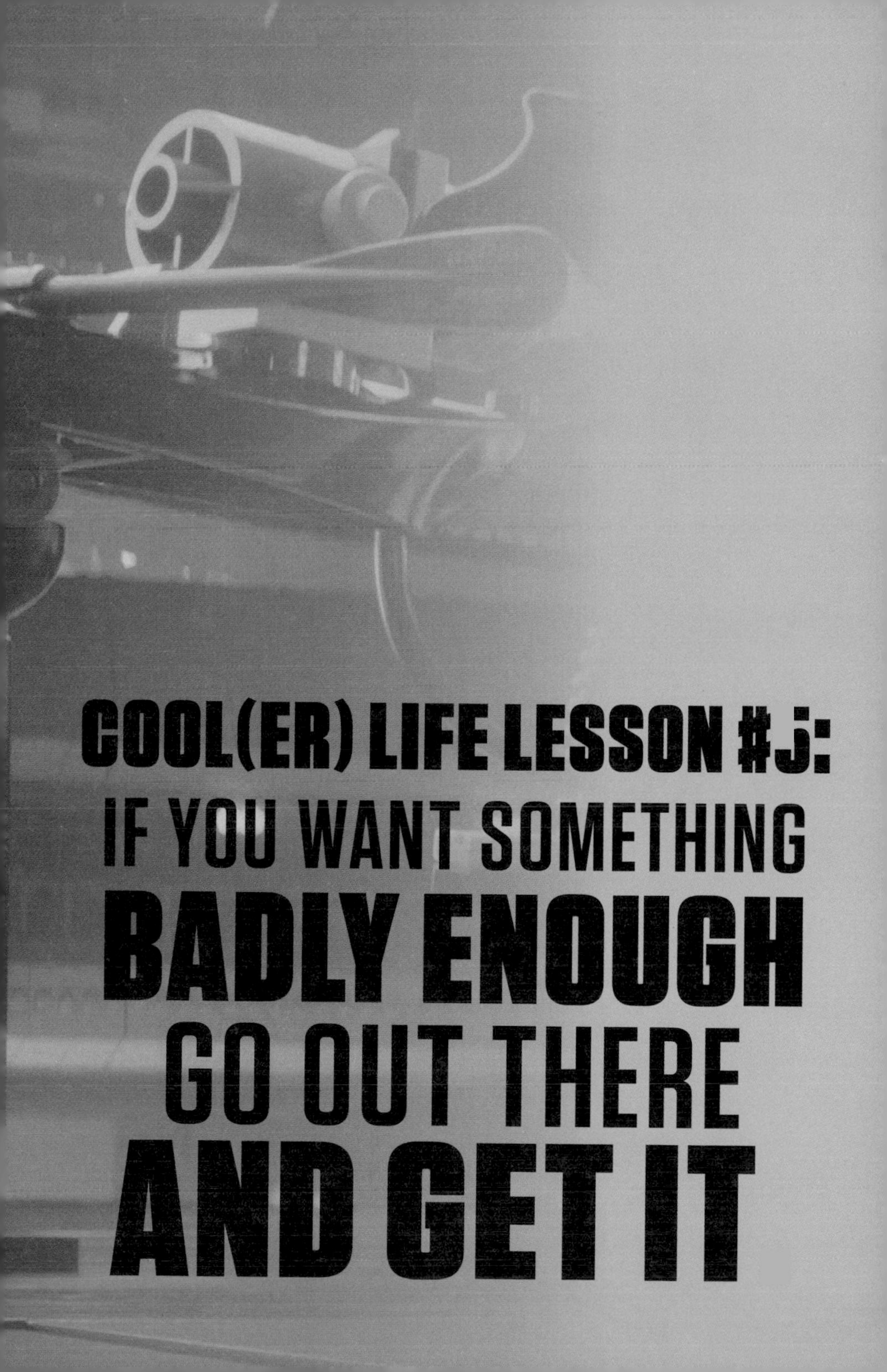

COOL(ER) LIFE LESSON #5:

IF YOU WANT SOMETHING BADLY ENOUGH GO OUT THERE AND GET IT

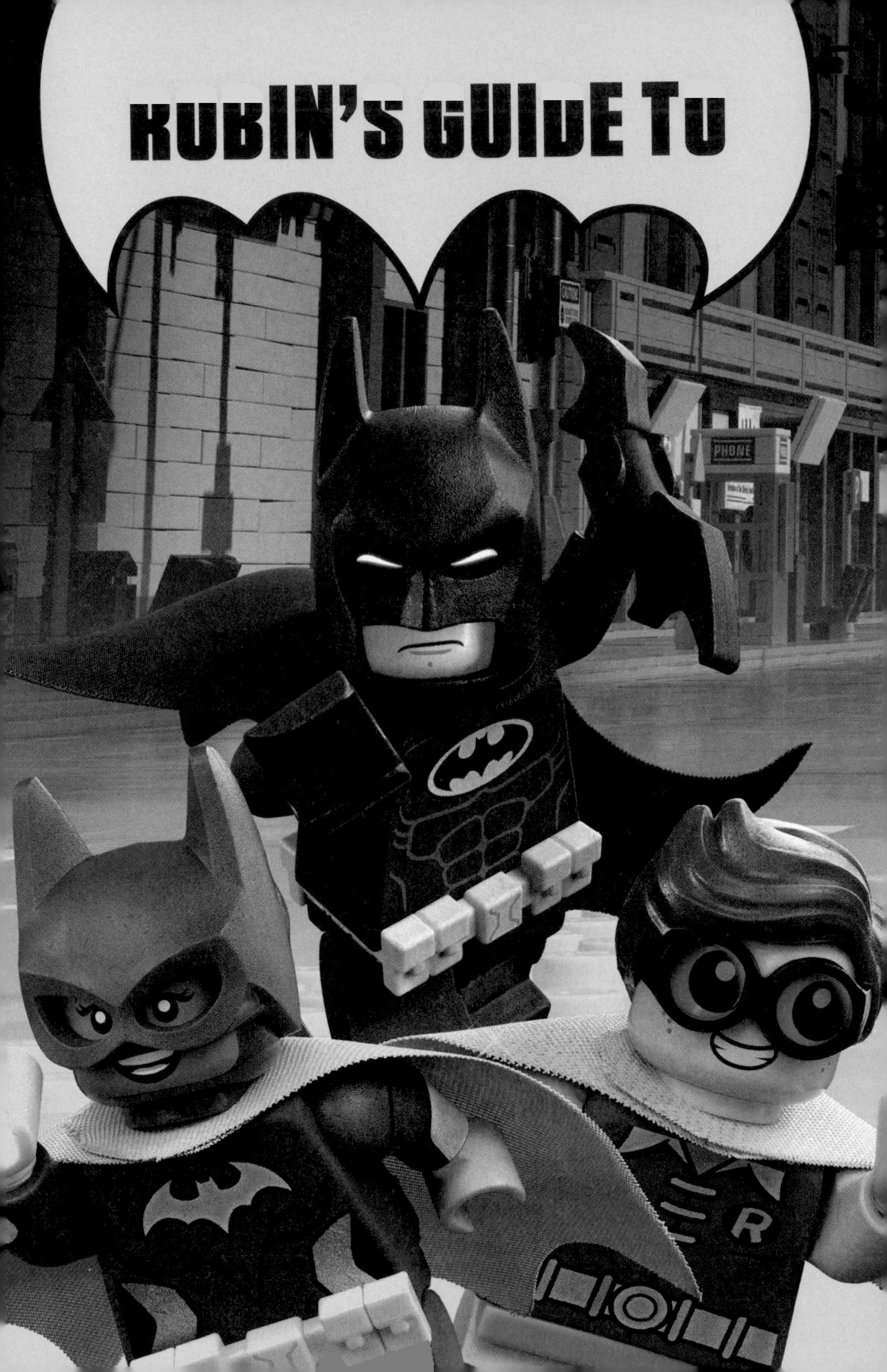
ROBIN'S GUIDE TO
PHONE

FOLLOWING
YOUR
DREAM

FLY, ROBIN, FLY

Can I tell you a secret? When I was at the orphanage, I kept the positivity vibe going by singing and dancing and nonstop gymnastics routines. But I was pretty lonely.

I mean, it gets a little boring singing your great new theme songs to yourself in the mirror. Every day.

All I ever wanted was a family of my own. And I was determined to make that dream come true no matter what!

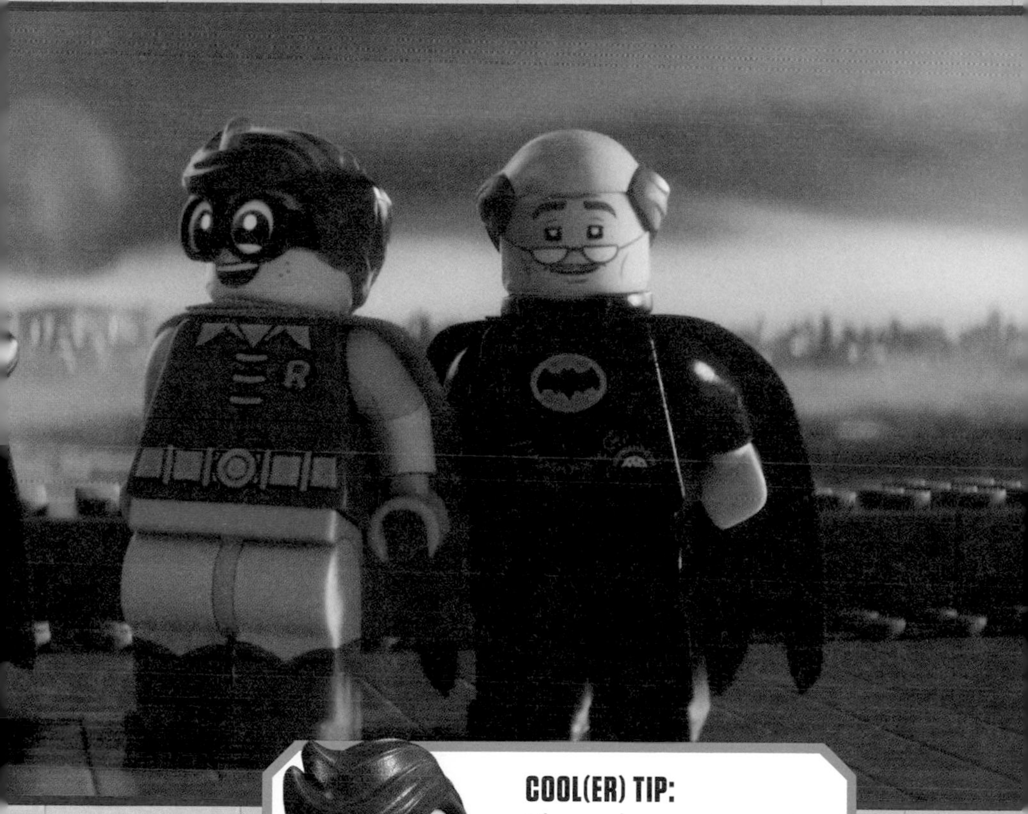

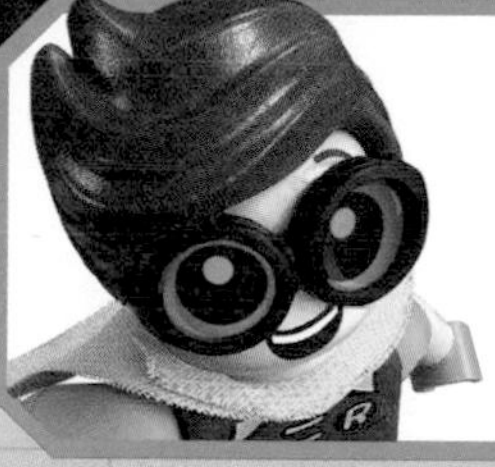

COOL(ER) TIP:
The only way to make your dreams come true is to go out there and chase them!

SAY CHEESE

One of my biggest dreams was to have a family photo. I know it doesn't seem like much. But gosh, those family photos are just so swell. They remind you of how special you are to your family, and how special they are to you!

Aw, man, just thinking about them gets the waterworks going. If my dad Batman were here right now, I bet he'd shed a lone tear of happiness. In a cool way.

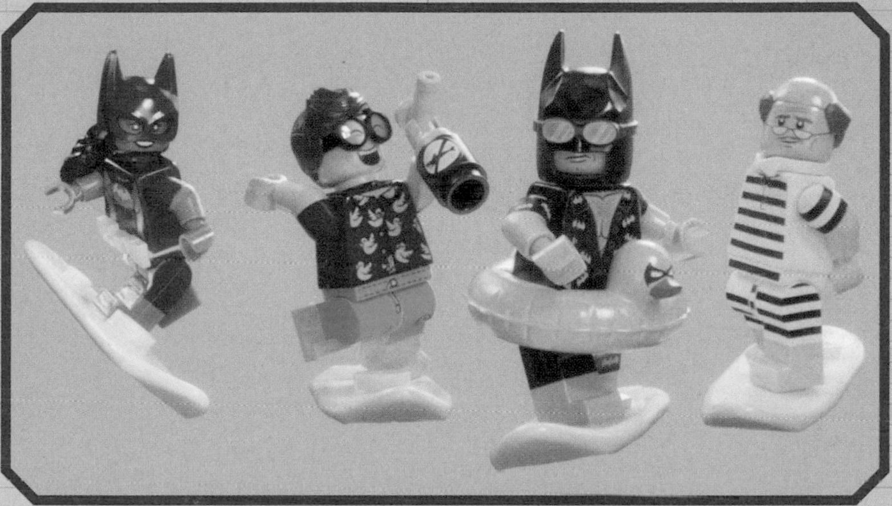

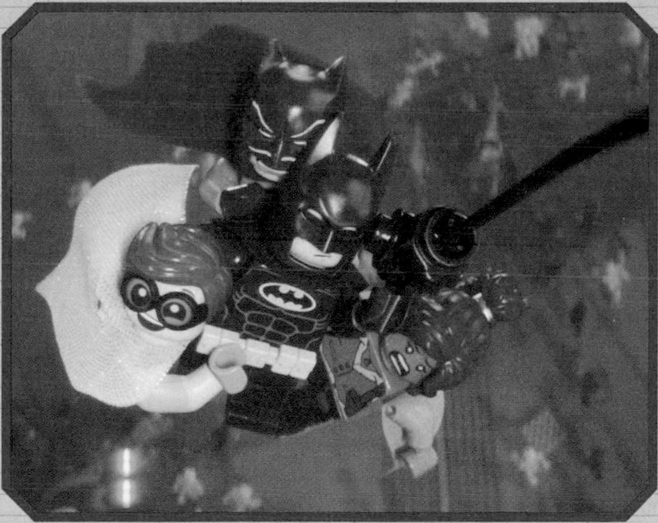

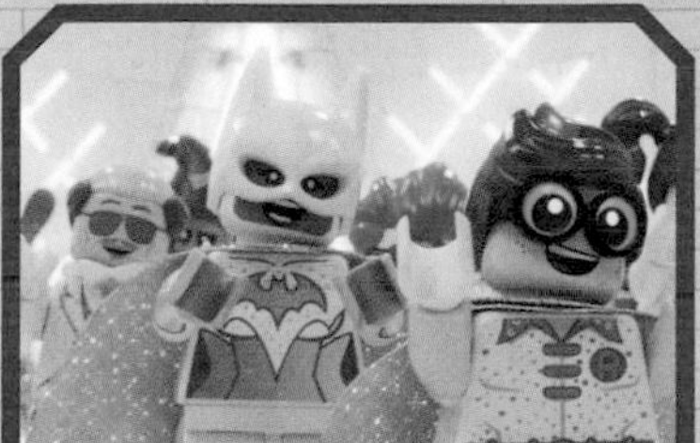

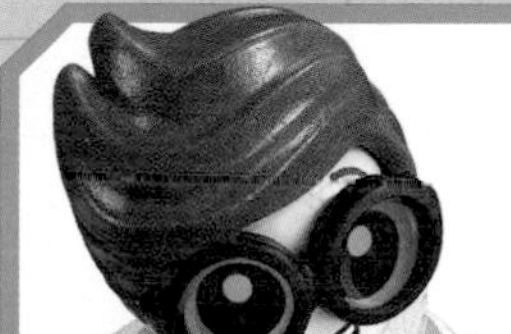

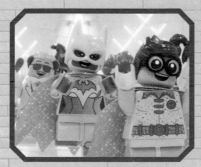

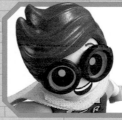

What's a cool(er) family photo that's special to you?

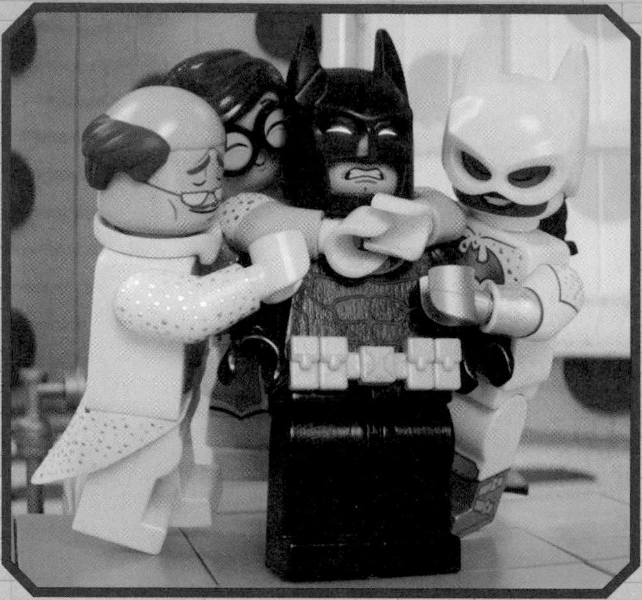

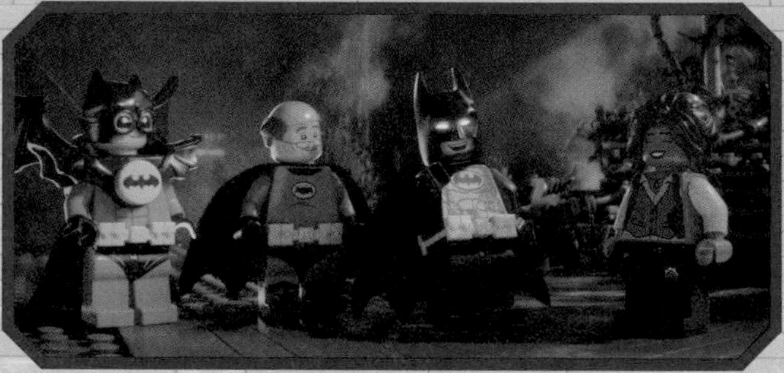

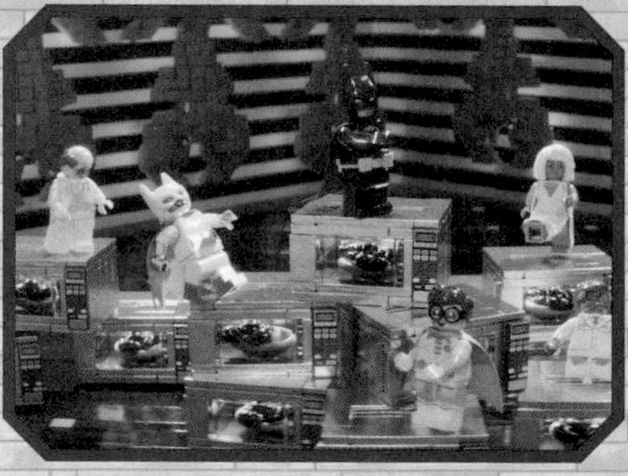

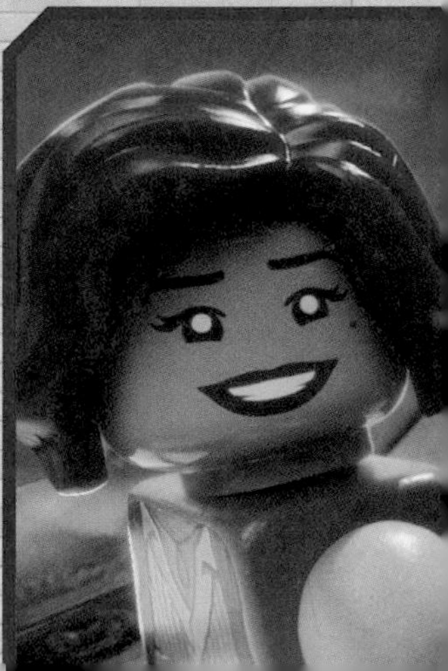

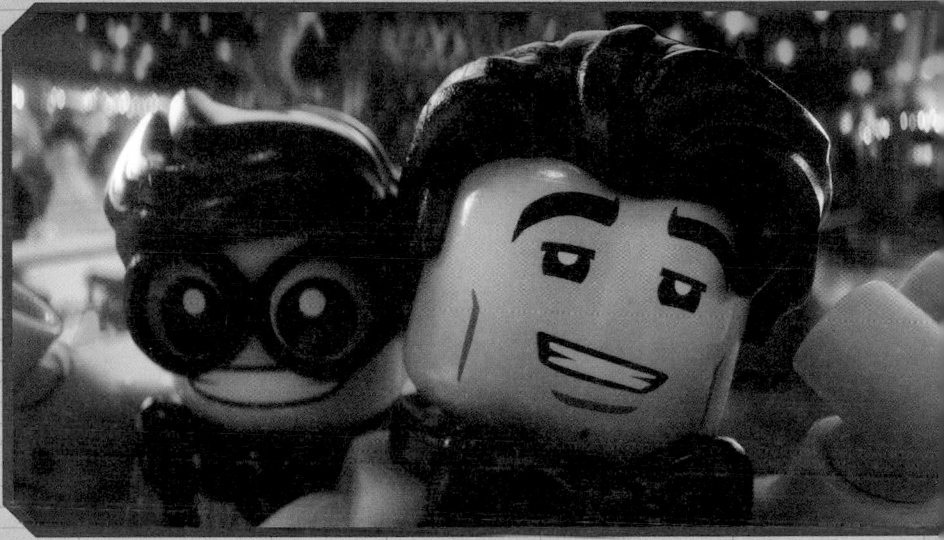

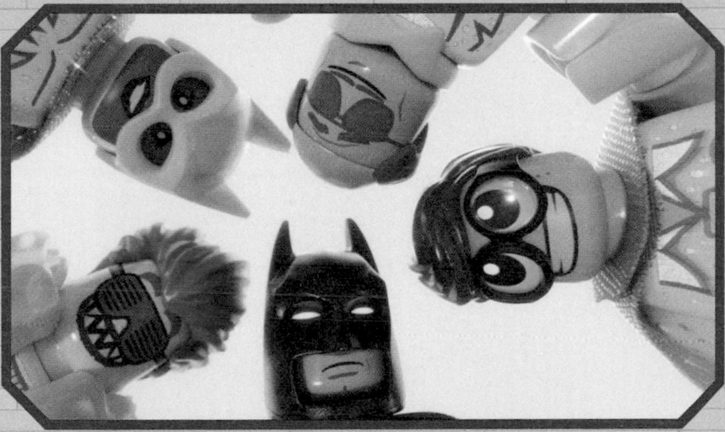

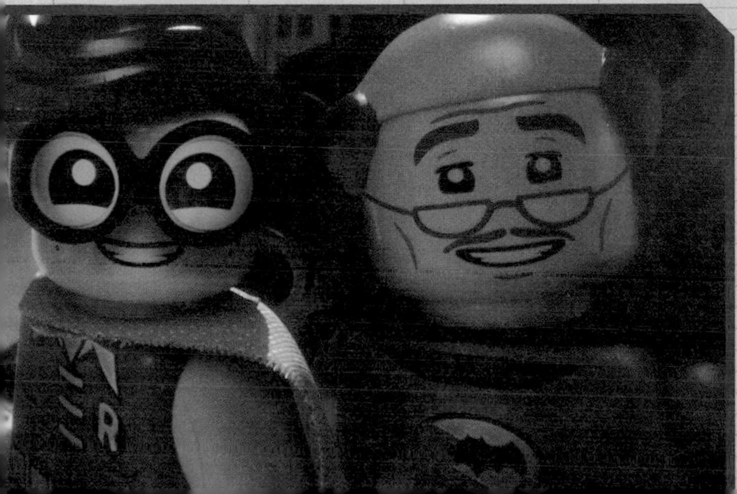

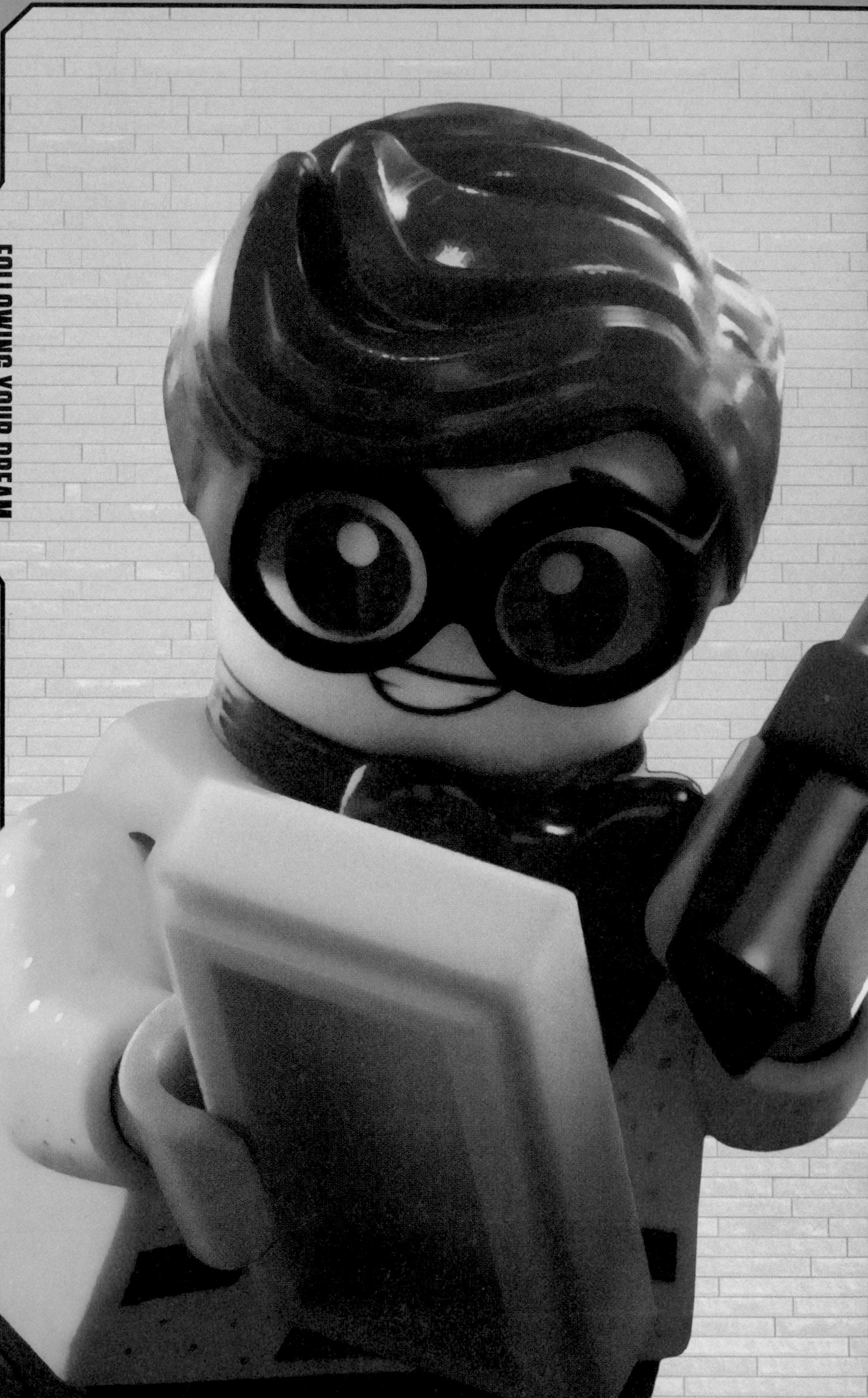

ROBIN'S TOP TEN WAYS FAMILY MAKES EVERYTHING COOL(ER)

1. Movie Nights

2. Family Dinner

3. Pillow Fights

4. Family Trips

5. Inside Jokes

6. Dress-Up Parties

7. Sing-Alongs

8. Silly Stories

9. Positive Parental Reinforcement

10. HUGS

COOL(ER) LIFE LESSON #6:

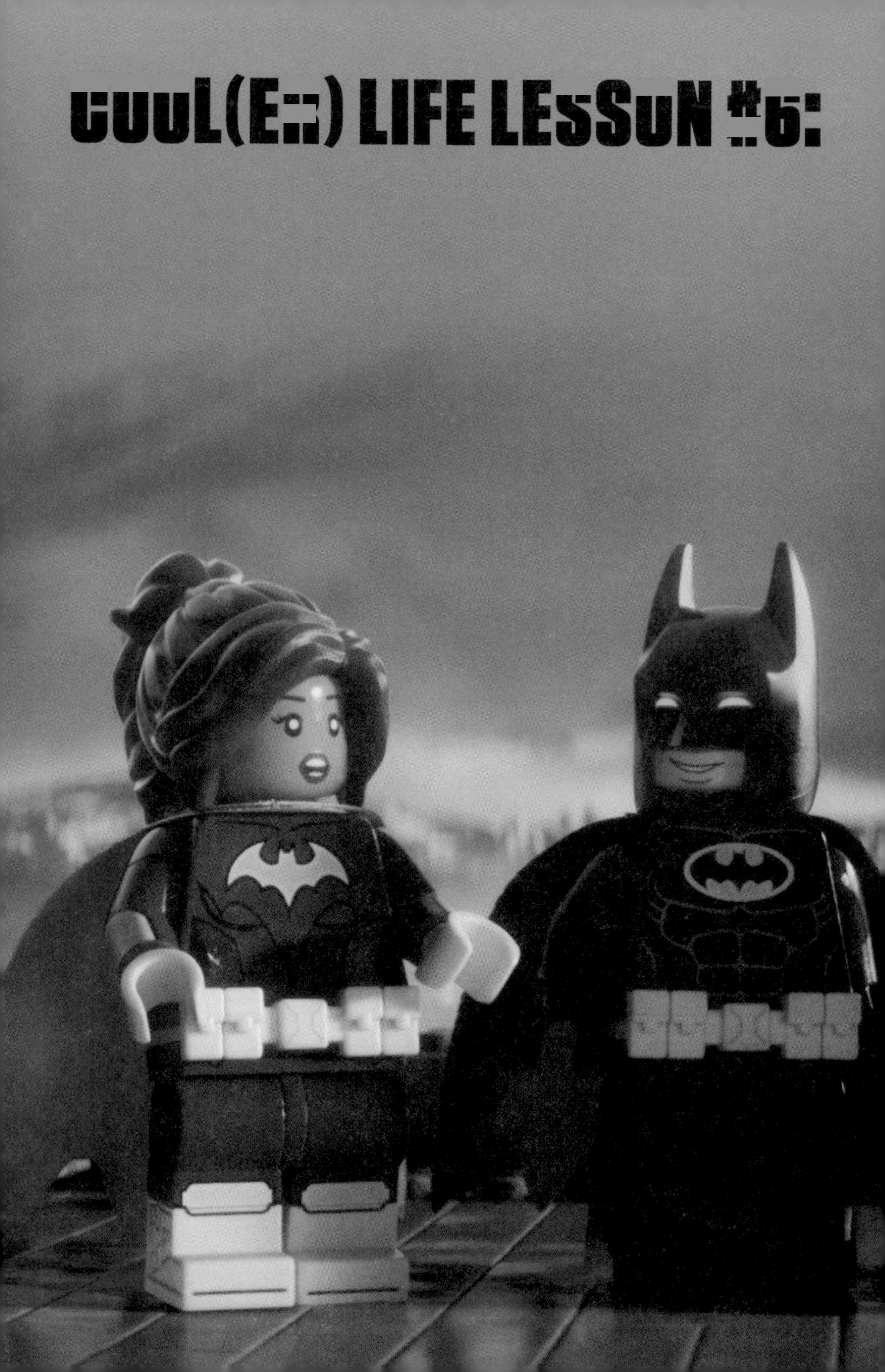

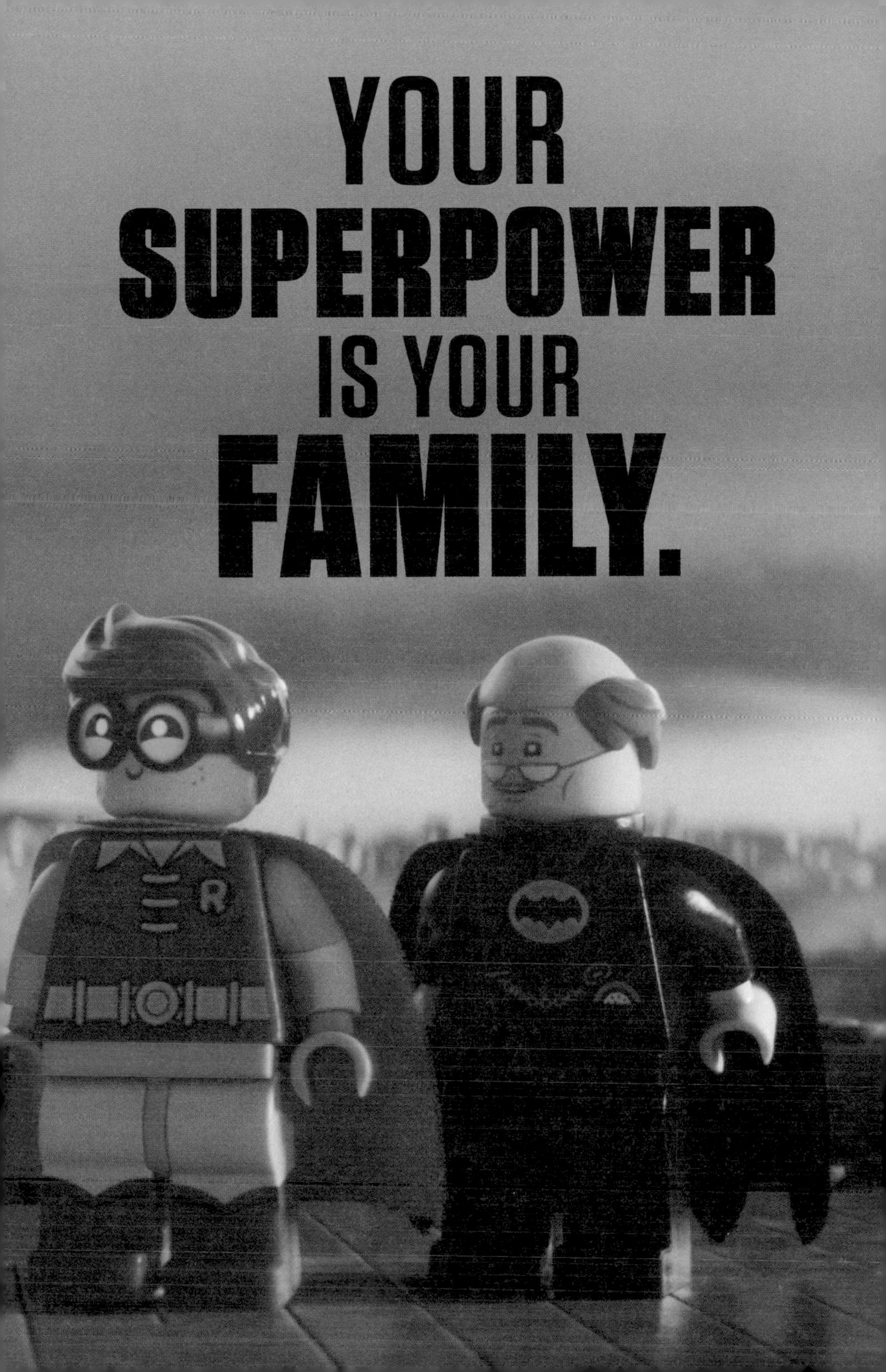
YOUR
SUPERPOWER
IS YOUR
FAMILY.
R

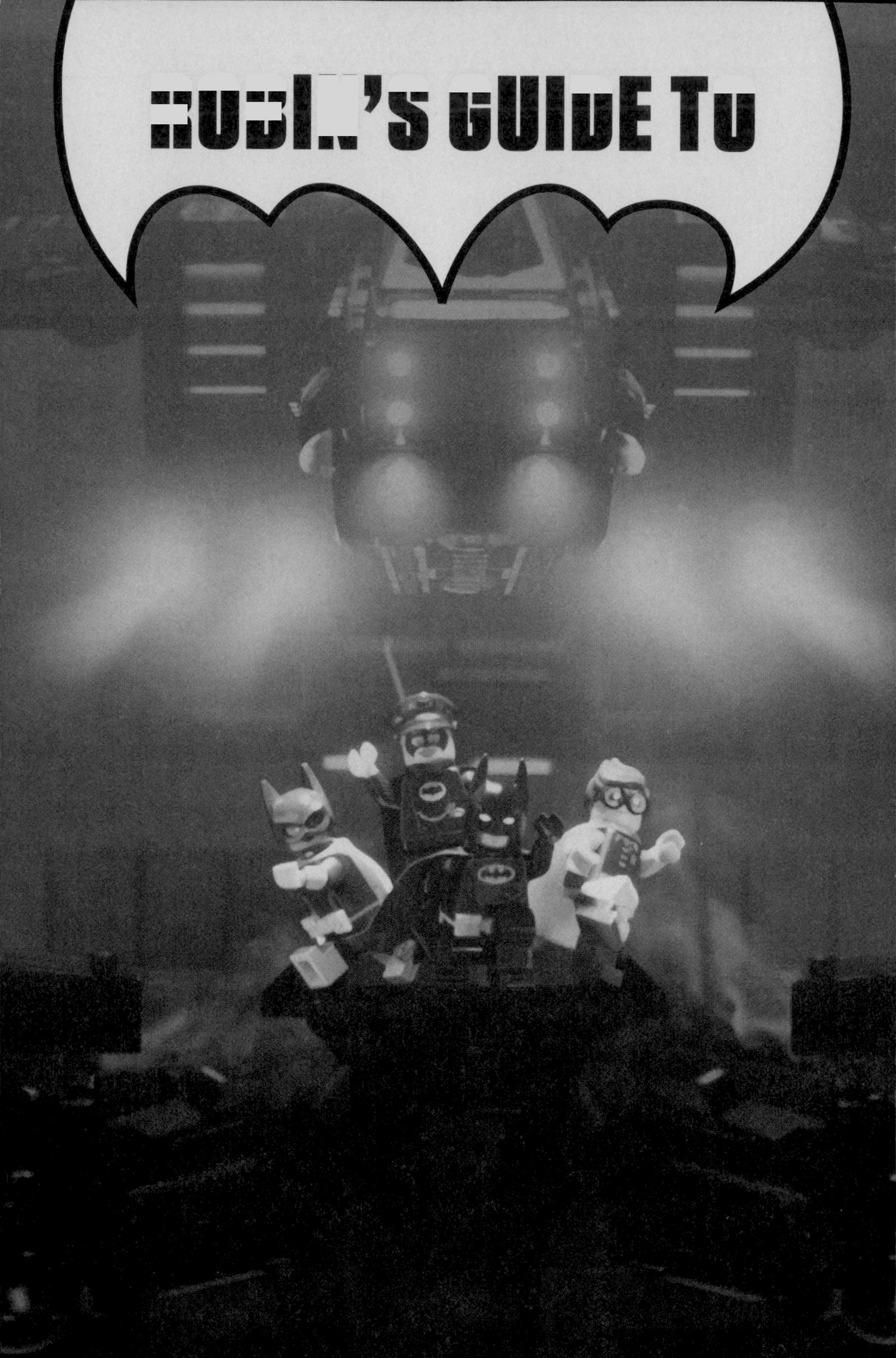
ROBIN'S GUIDE TO

BEING A COOL(ER) FAMILY

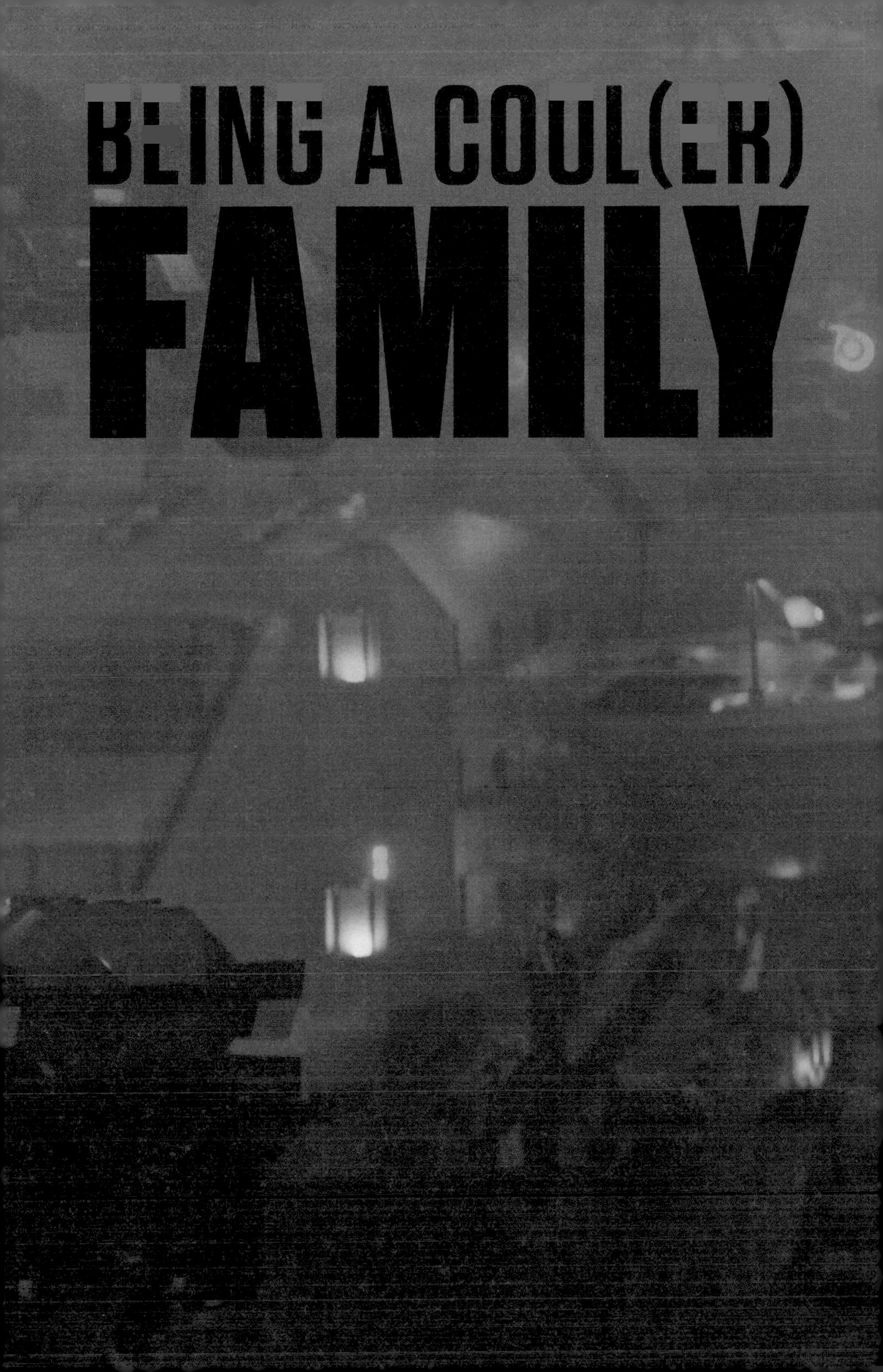

BAT-PARENTING

Your family has so much to teach you! That's what makes them cool(er). Batman totally parented me during our missions, and it was awesome. I just love being parented!

SEE? SCARED . . .

NOT SCARED!

BAT-PARENTING SUCCESS!

BAT-DAD LESSON #1:

When the mega-bad guys came to take over the city, I was a little scared. But my *padre* taught me it's okay to be scared. Even he gets scared sometimes! (Shhhh—I'm pretty sure that's a secret.) But do you know what Batman does when he's scared? He beatboxes those fears away!

BAT-DAD LESSON #2:

Batman totally taught me to drive. Well, he taught me to drive *after* I kind of blew up the Batmobile. But better late than never, right? Yeah!

BAT-PARENTING
COMPLETE!

BAT-DAD LESSON #3:

He even put me in a time-out when I wasn't following his instructions. Cool!

YOU'VE JUST BEEN BAT-PARENTED!

WE ARE FAMILY

And you know what? I taught Batman a thing or two about being part of a family, too. (I know, right? How cool(er) is that!?)

You see, Batman wasn't 100 percent sure he was ready to be in a family again. But anyone can be a family. It's just about finding the people you care about, and who care about you.

Alfred is Batman's butler. But he's been like a father to him for many years. So he's basically Batman's dad in the ways that really count.

≥OLDER≤
FATHER

Obviously, Batman is the coolest dad ever.

And then there's me! Even though we're not technically related, I'm still 100 percent his son. Because friends are the family that you can choose, and Batman chose ME! I just love my *padre* so much!

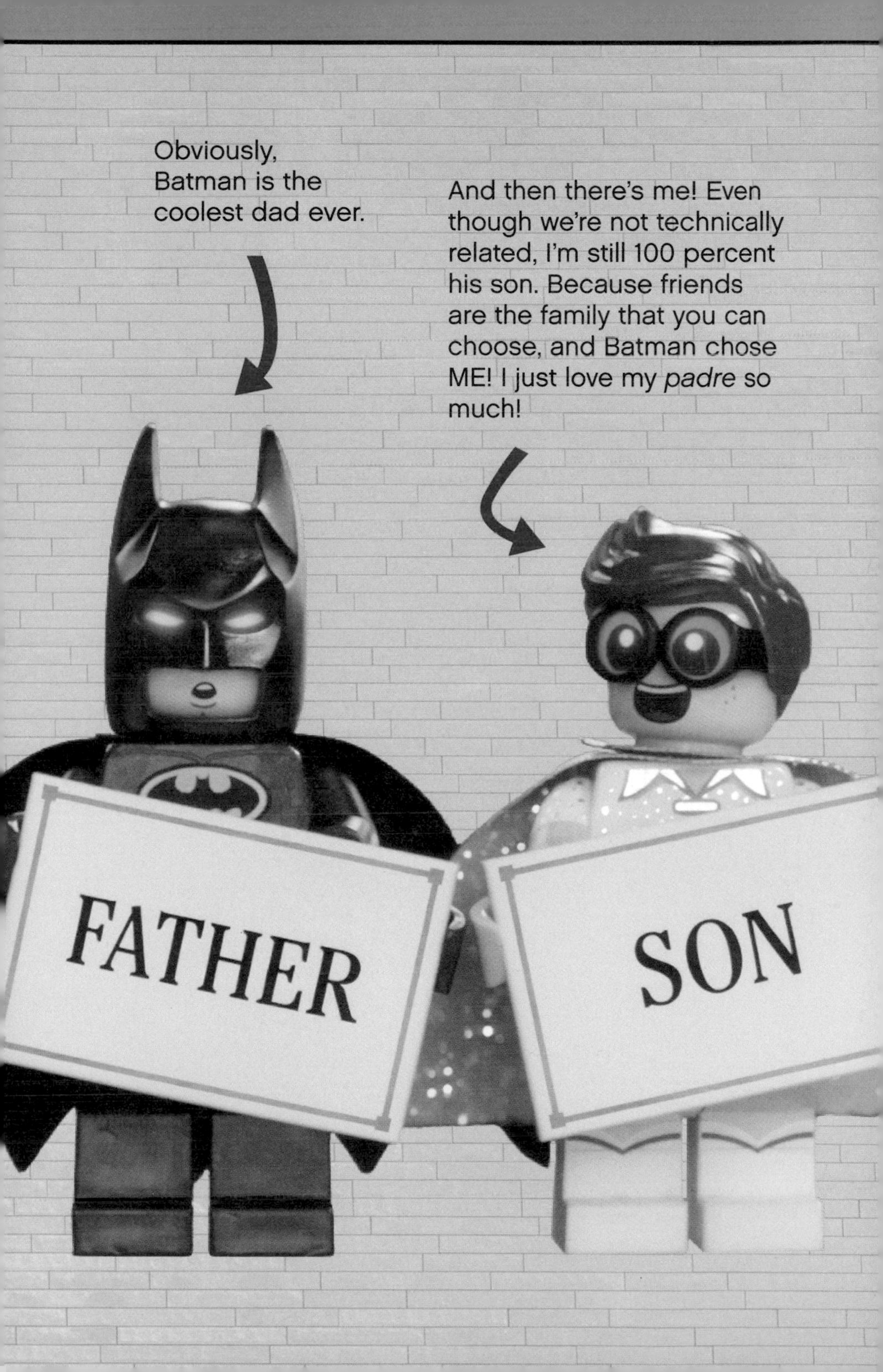
FATHER
SON

THE BAD GUY BUNCH

Even super-villains can be family! Hey, everybody is *somebody's* someone, right? And these guys are like several dozen pillagers in a pod.

Father

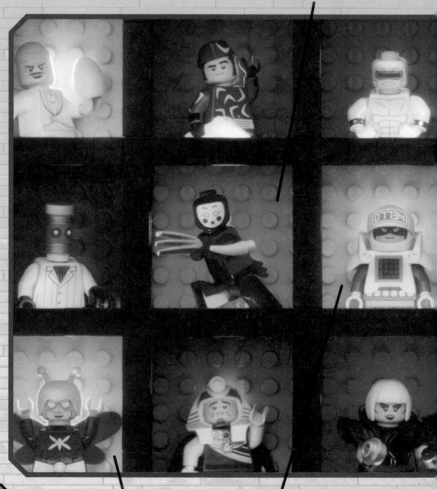

Daughter

Cousin

Grandparent

Mother

Aunt

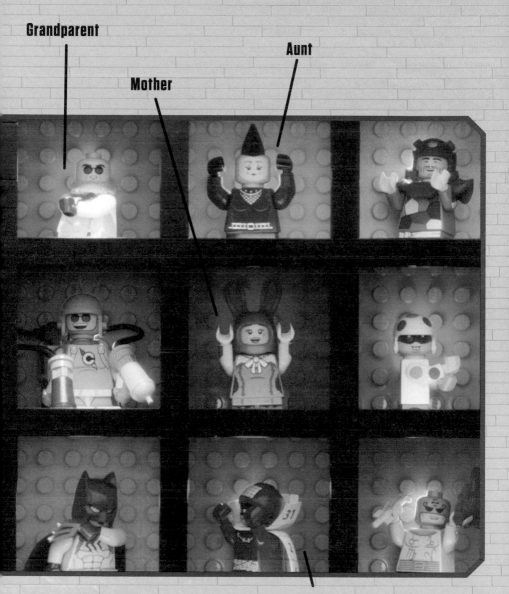

Son

H-U-G

But what's most important is that families never give up on one another. Even when you're scared, or when bad things happen, you need to be there for your family. A big old hug goes a long way.

Sometimes people will make you sad. But that's okay. It doesn't mean you stop letting them in. Someone very wise taught me that—my dad.

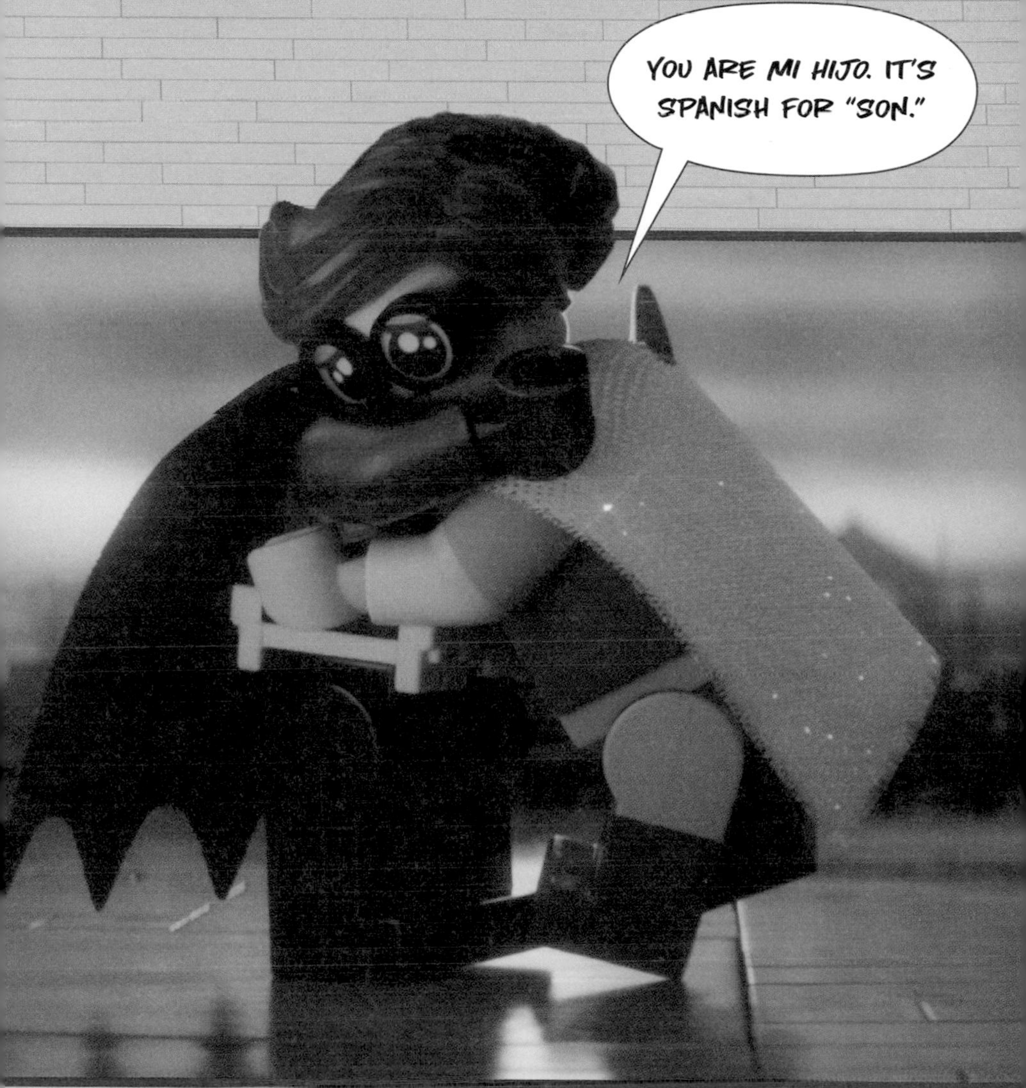
YOU ARE MI HIJO. IT'S SPANISH FOR "SON."

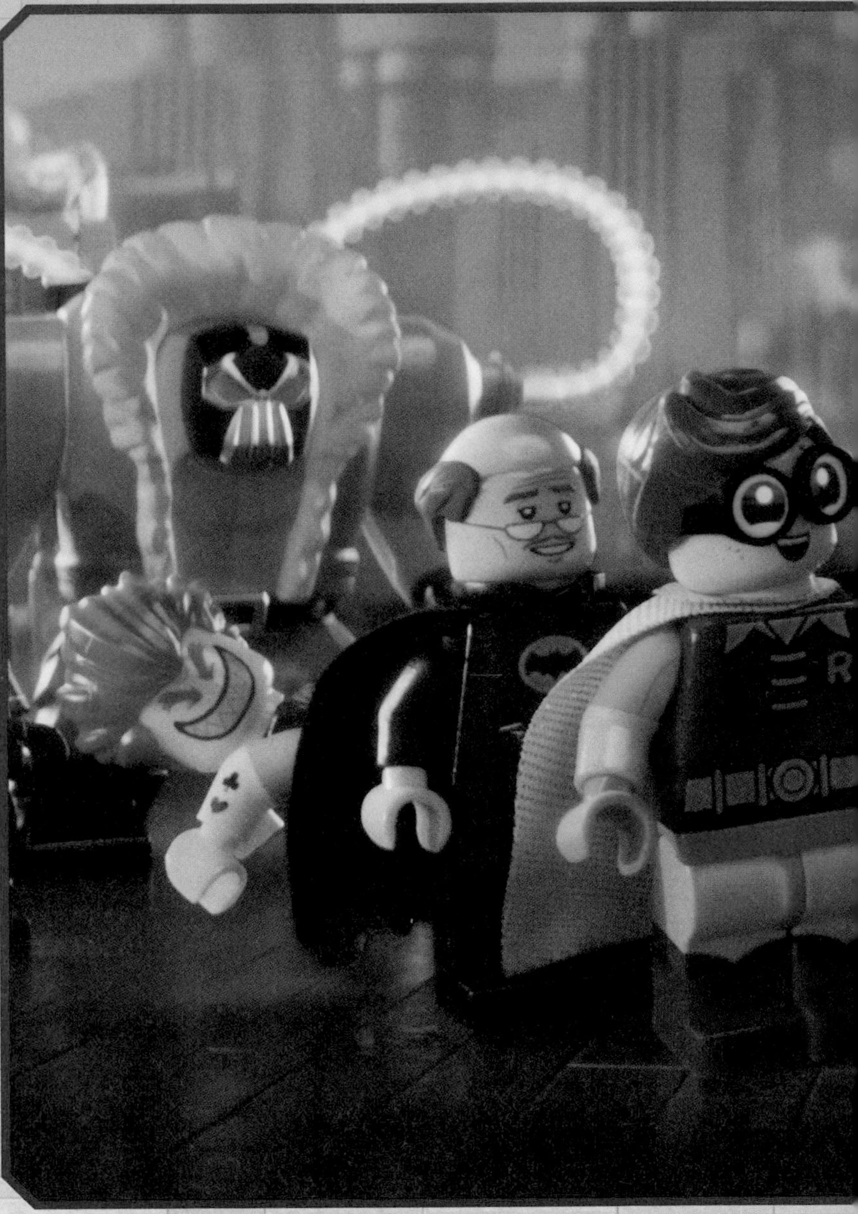
R

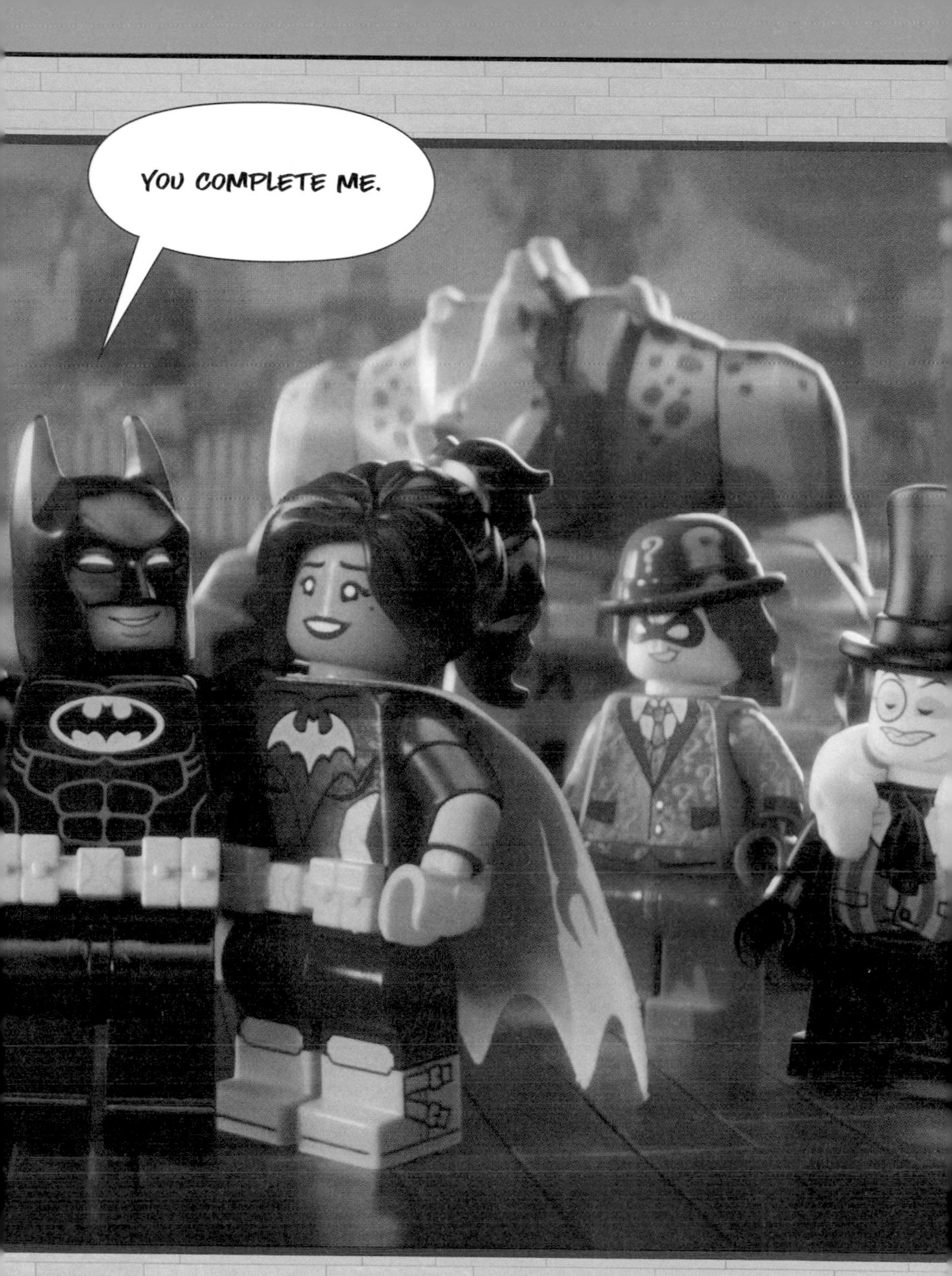
YOU COMPLETE ME.

COOL(ER) LIFE LESSON #7:
YOU CAN NEVER GET
ENOUGH HUGS.

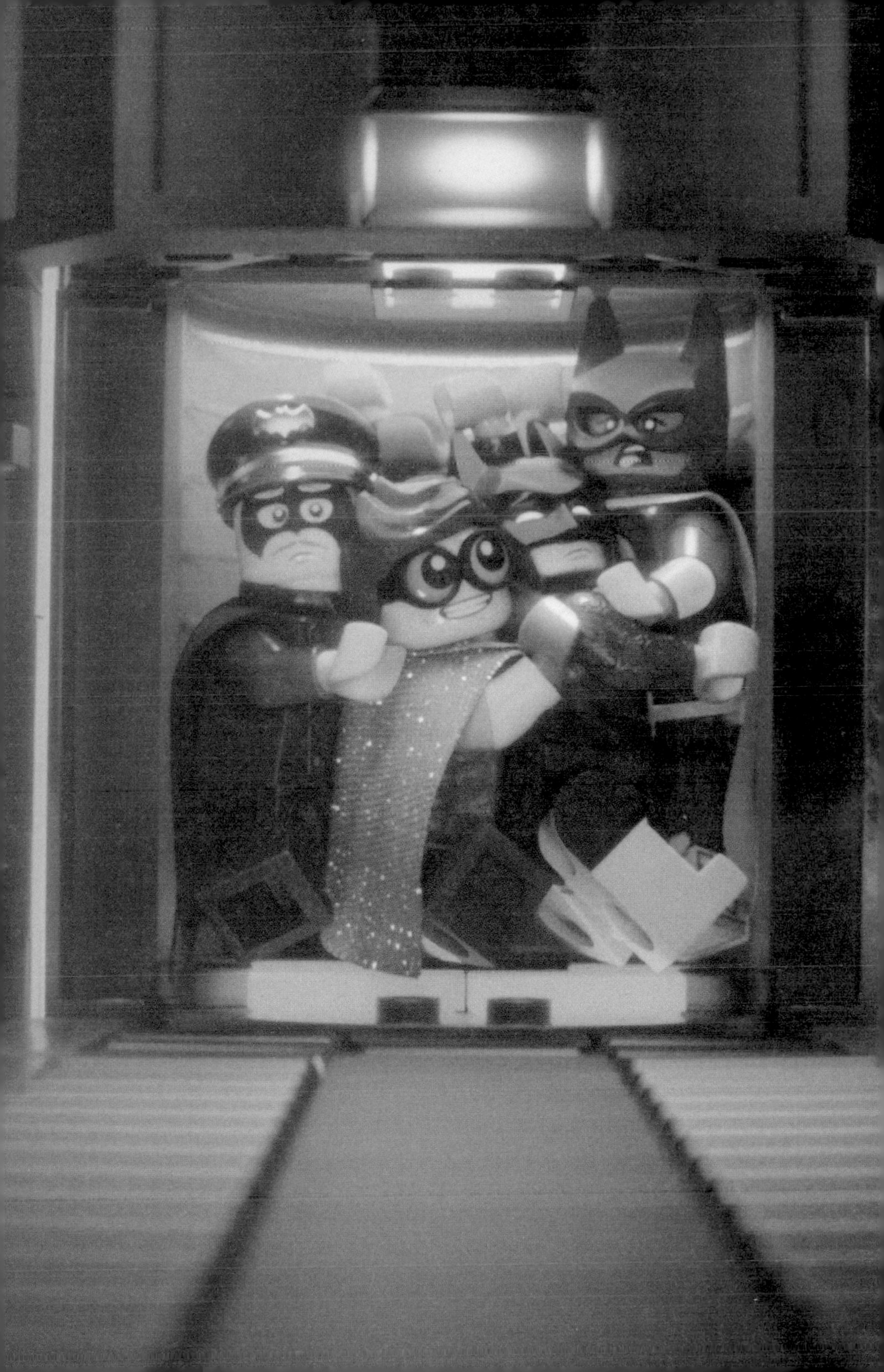

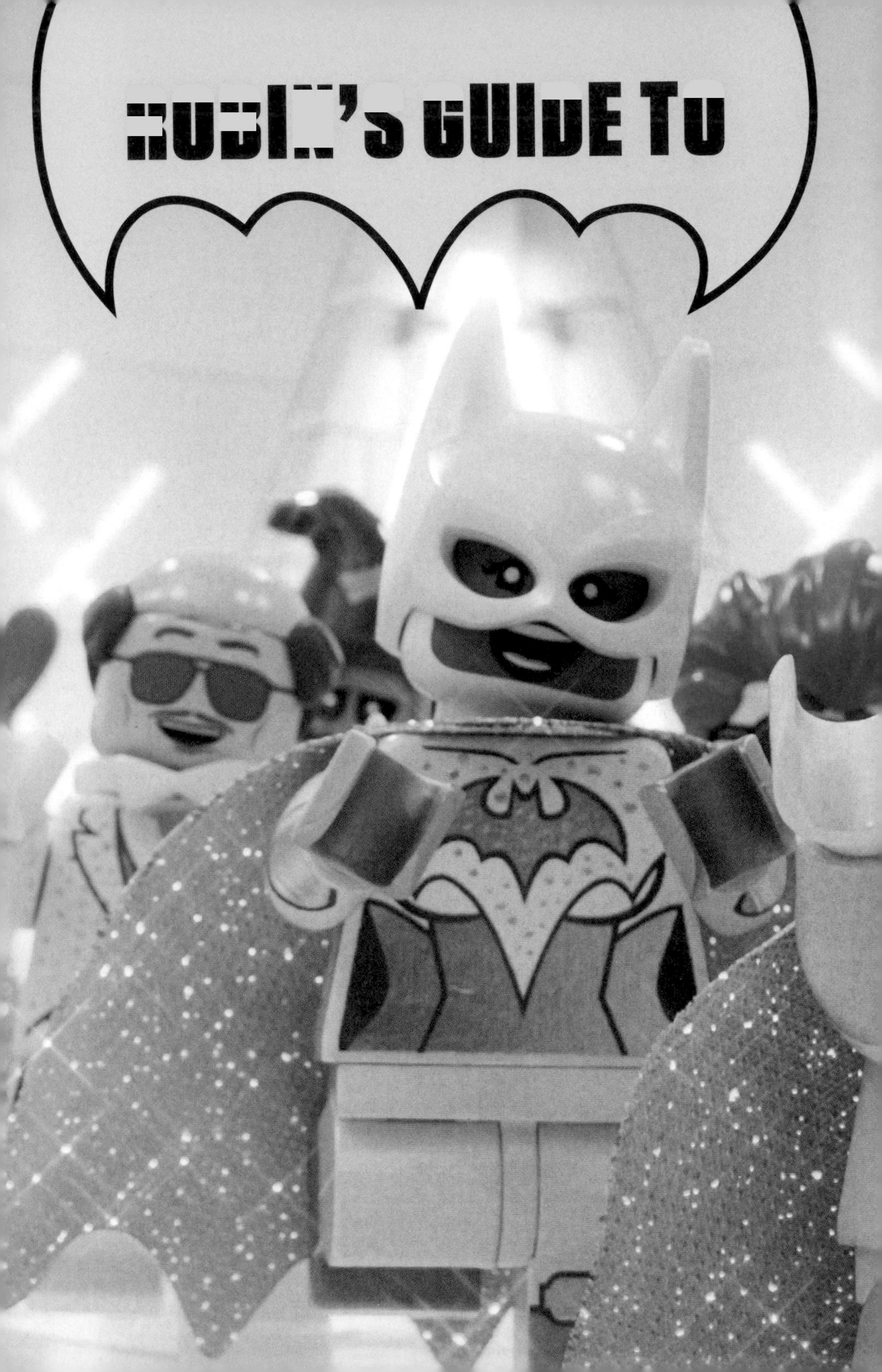
ROBIN'S GUIDE TO

GROOVY SING-ALONGS

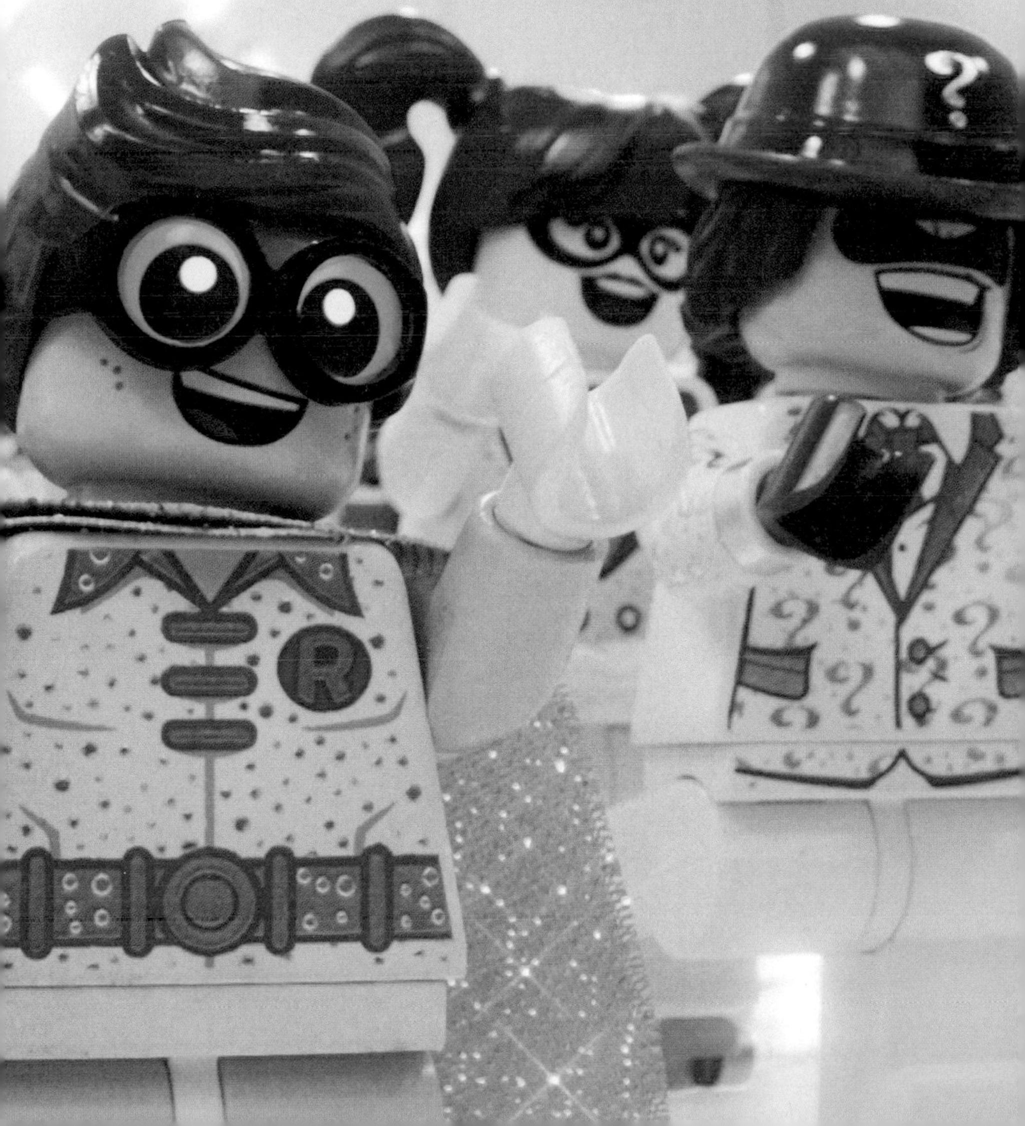

GET UP EVERYBODY AND SING!

Okay, enough with the mushy-gushy feely feels. It's time to get up and get grooving! It's a proven fact that the family that sings together stays together. And boy, oh, boy, do I like to SING! It's one of my special abilities. As special as a superpower! I just have an uncanny knack for picking the right music for any occasion.

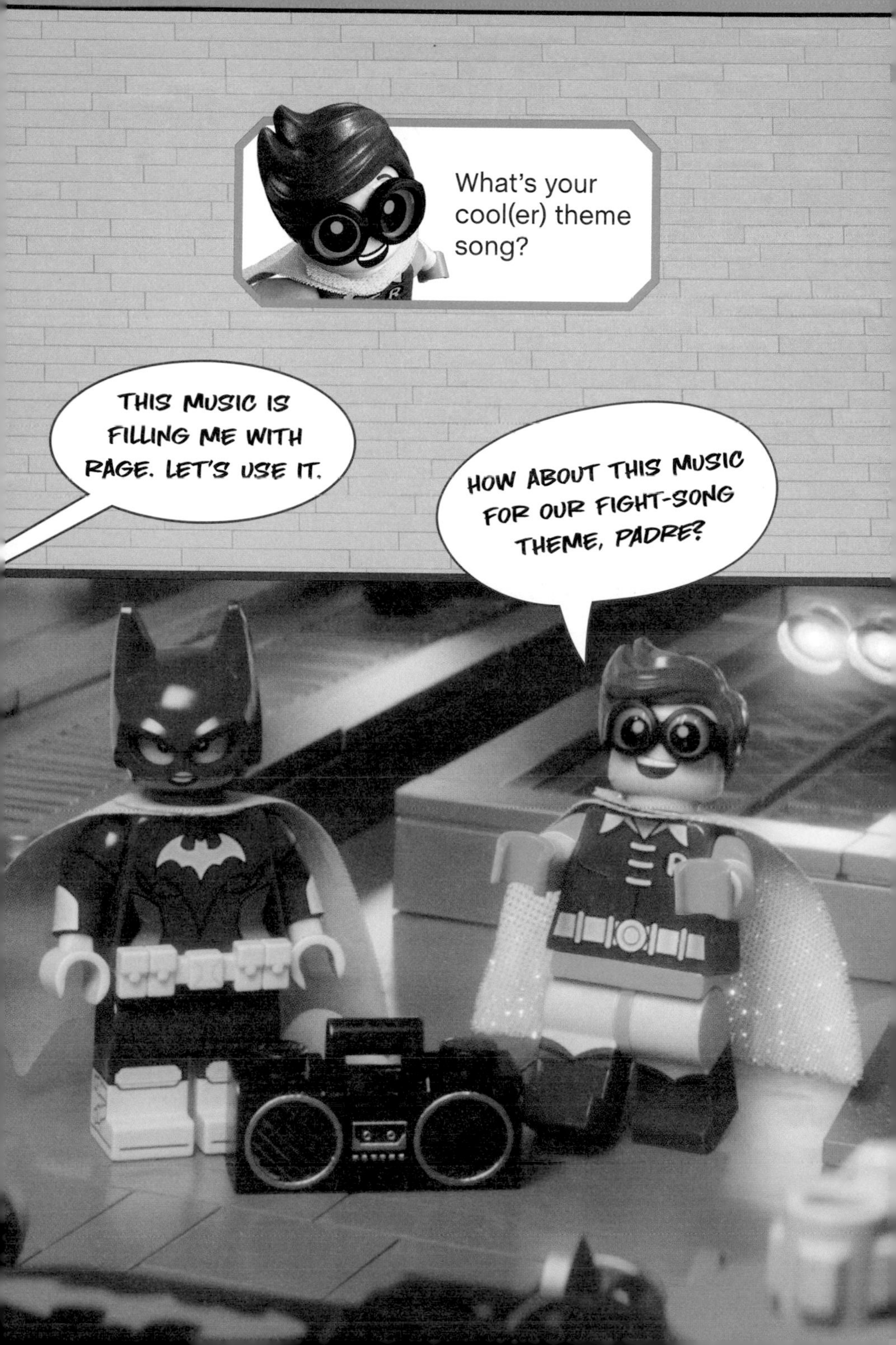
What's your cool(er) theme song?
THIS MUSIC IS FILLING ME WITH RAGE. LET'S USE IT.
HOW ABOUT THIS MUSIC FOR OUR FIGHT-SONG THEME, PADRE?

FAMILY THEME SONG

Check out this cool(er) theme song that I wrote especially for my family!

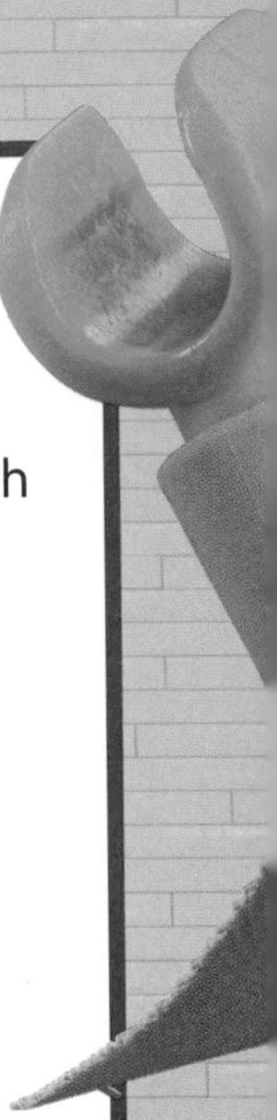

I wake up early in the morning
and I'm texting you.
(Hey, Robin, it's 7:30!)

Well, that's okay, I'm ready to fight crime with
you, the Dark Knight.
(I'll be sleeping past 2:00.)

We sometimes fight. (BOOM, POW, BANG!)

But we always make up.
(Hey, man, I'm sorry. It's okay. Okay!)

We're not related, but here's good news:

Friends are the family you can choose.

High-five. Down low. To the side. Let's go!

You're my best friend, my best friend,
and friends are family.

You're my best friend, my best friend,
and friends are family.

You're my family.
Come on everybody and sing!

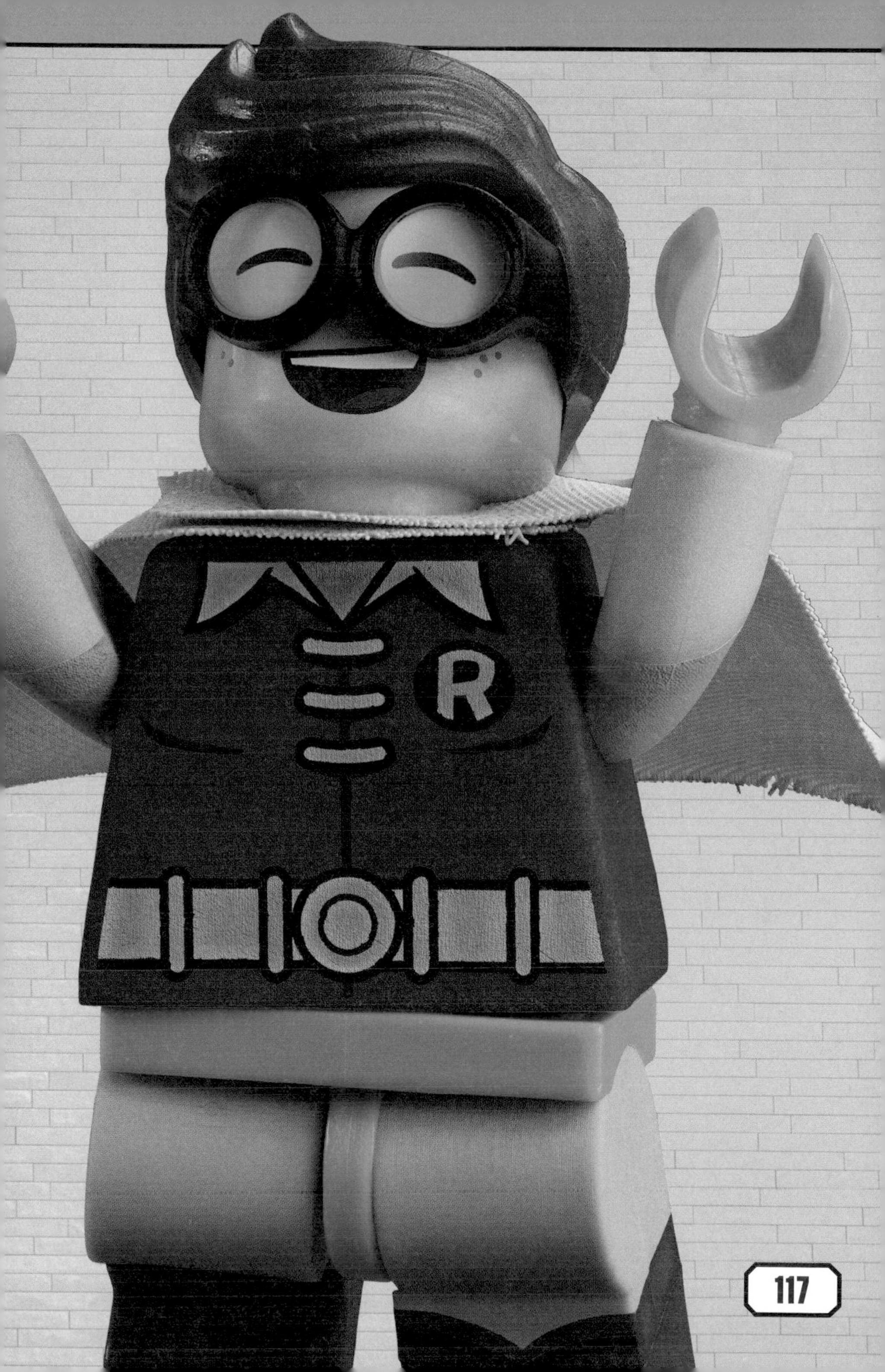
R

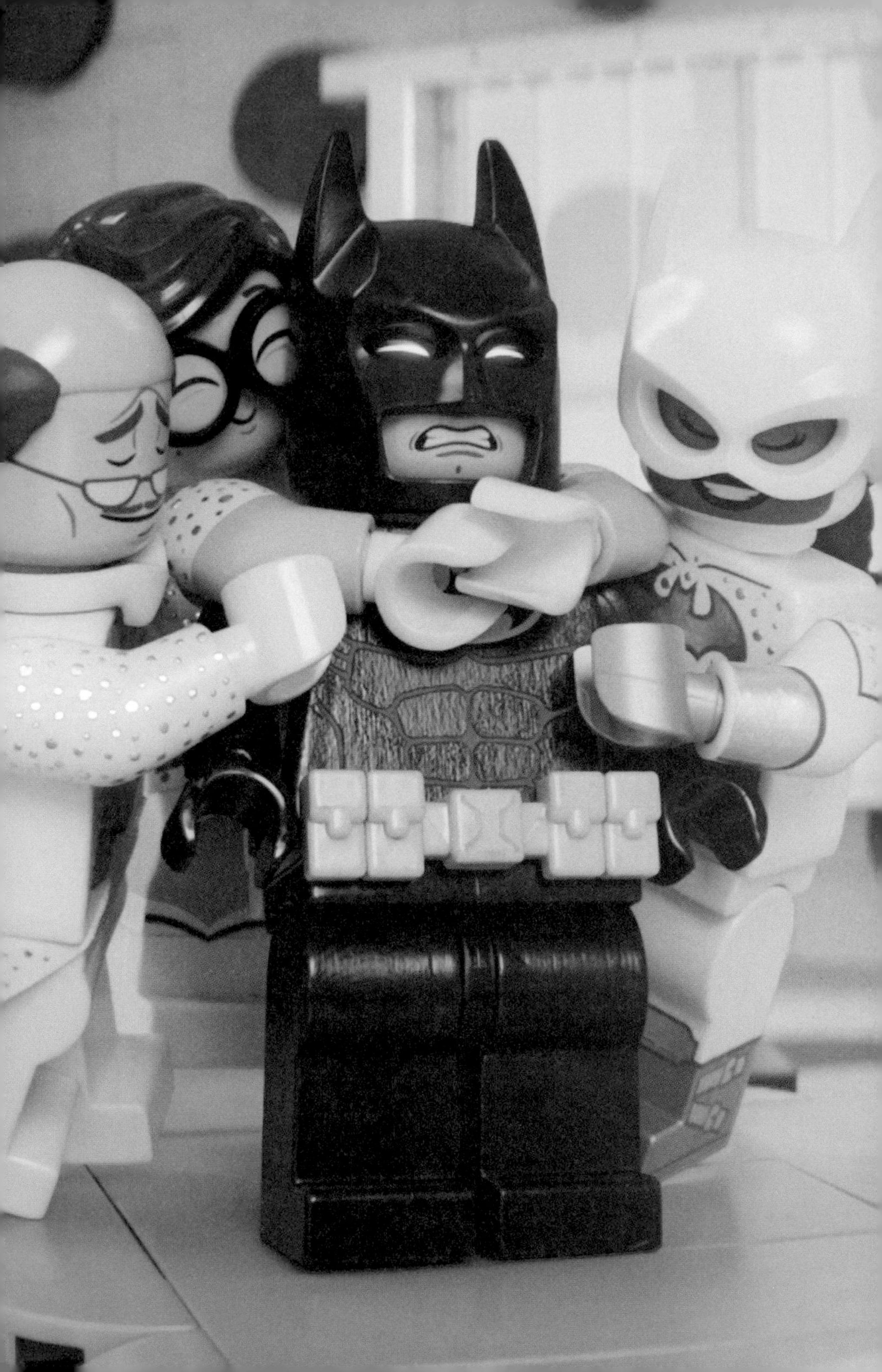

COOL(ER) LIFE LESSON #8:
FRIENDS
ARE
FAMILY!

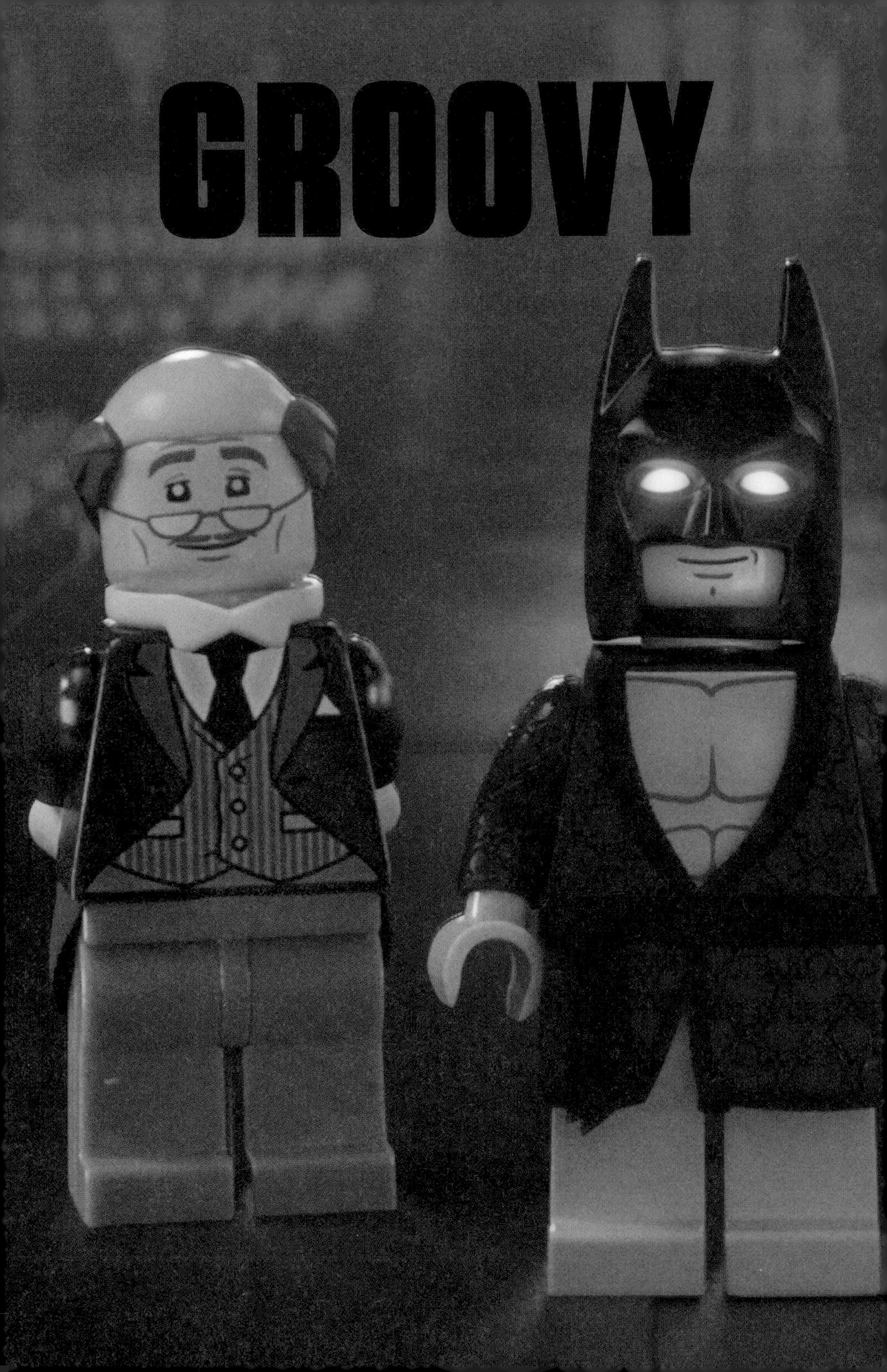
GROOVY

GOOD-BYE

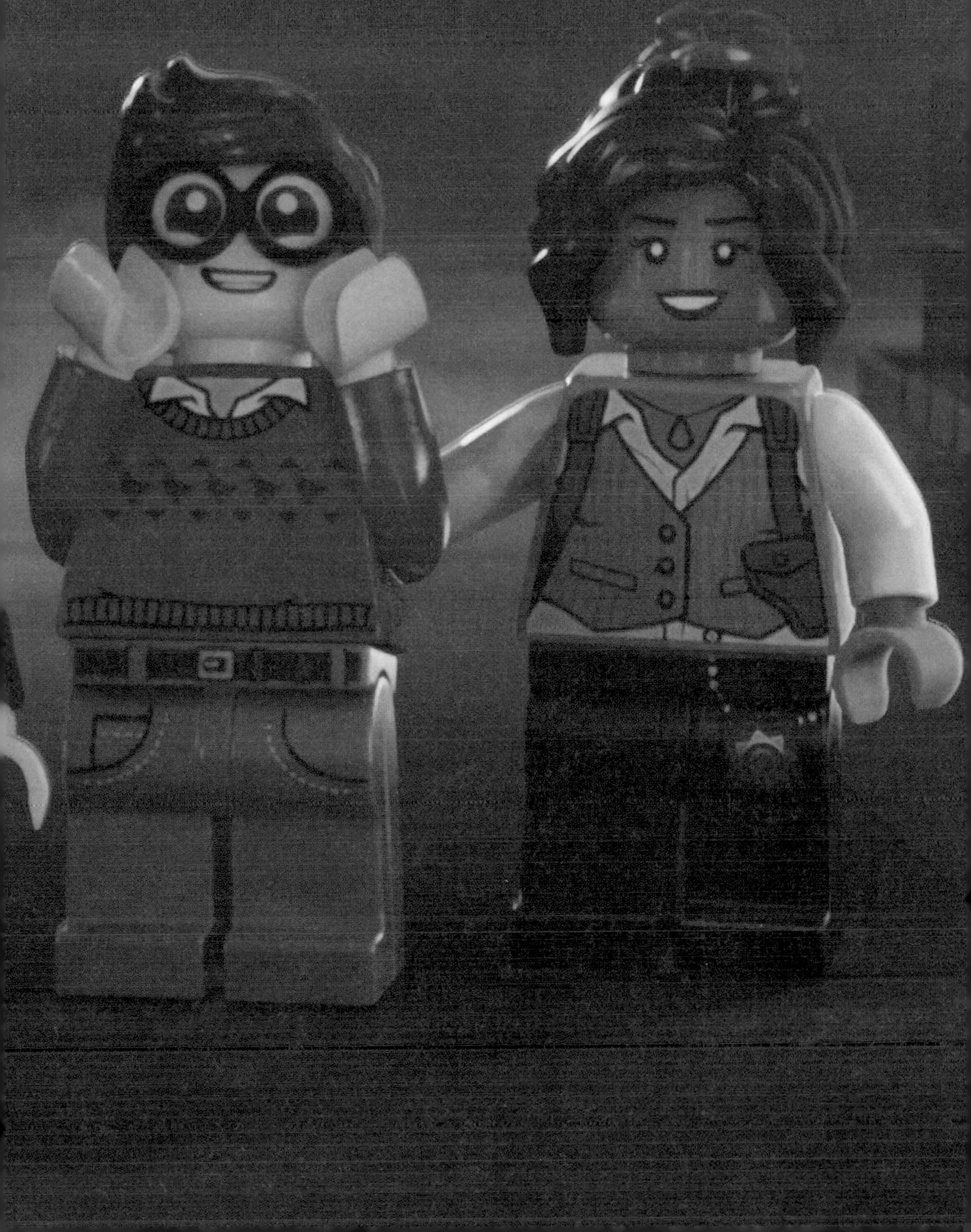

TIME TO FLY AND SAY GOOD-BYE

Well, gosh, thanks so much for reading this book. It sure has been swell sharing all the tips I've learned for being cool(er). Oh, oh! And now that I've taught you everything I've learned, maybe you could show me your own ways of being cool(er)? Hot diggity dog! Here are some ideas to get you started!

1. Create your own Super Hero costume.
Let your inner creativity pour out and design the costume you feel like you were poured into.

2. Invent a secret Super Hero code. Nothing says "cool(er)" than a secret code to use with your friends so you can communicate on the down low. When you desire to.

3. Go on a "helping" mission. Your friends are like your family. So, show them you care by lending a helping hand!

4. Try a new hobby. Driftwood art and kendo-stick routines are always nifty party tricks.

5. Compose your own theme song. Life is cool(er) when you have a groovy soundtrack to get down to.

6. Draw a family portrait. A hand-drawn portrait of your number-one peeps is sure to warm your family's heart.

7. Come up with a super-secret handshake. Then practice it with your friends, your siblings, even your neighbors. Bonus points if it ends in a hug!

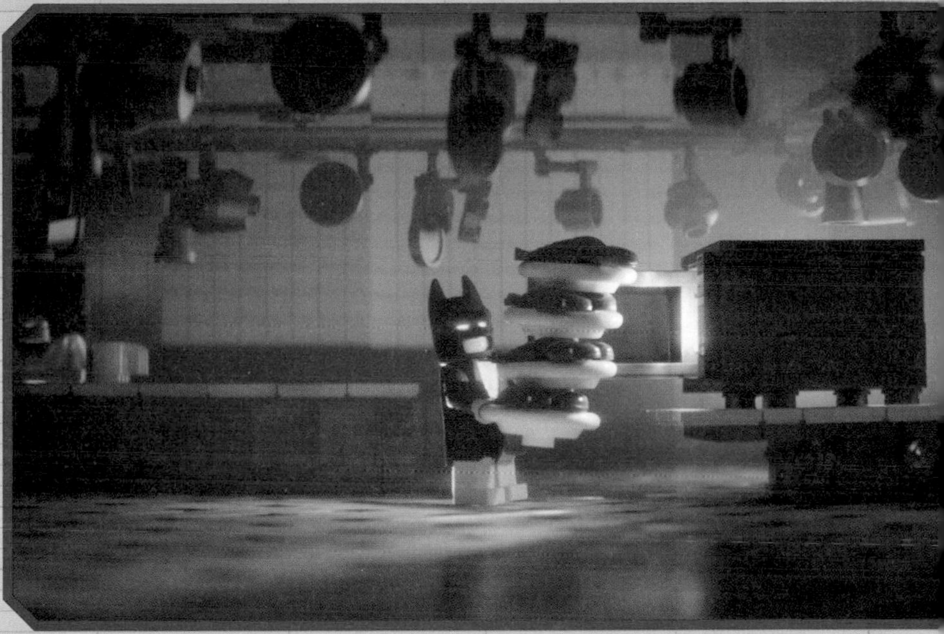

8. Invent a Super Hero recipe. Show off those mad cooking skills. Super Heroes can't fight on an empty stomach.

9. Write a story about your dream goal. Who knows? One day, your story may become reality!

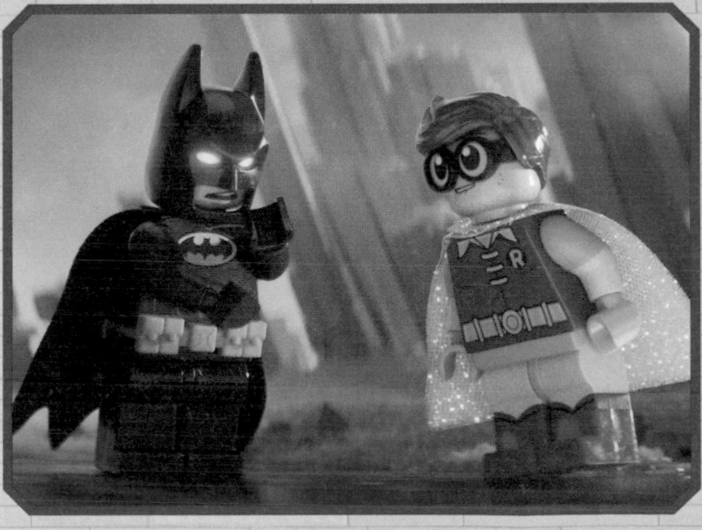

10. Tell your family you love them. 24/7, 365 days, at a million percent. Trust me on this one. It's worth it.

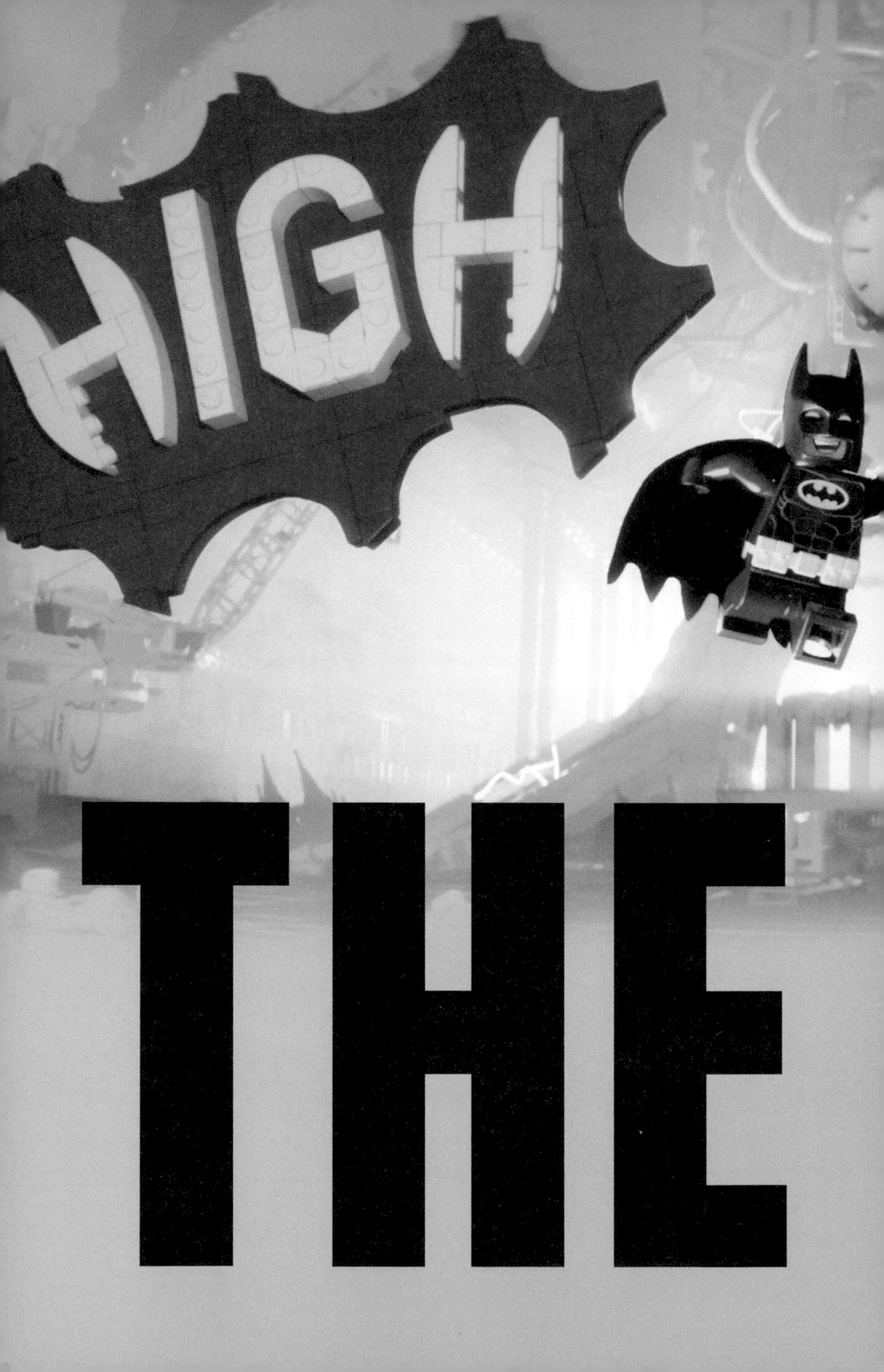
THE

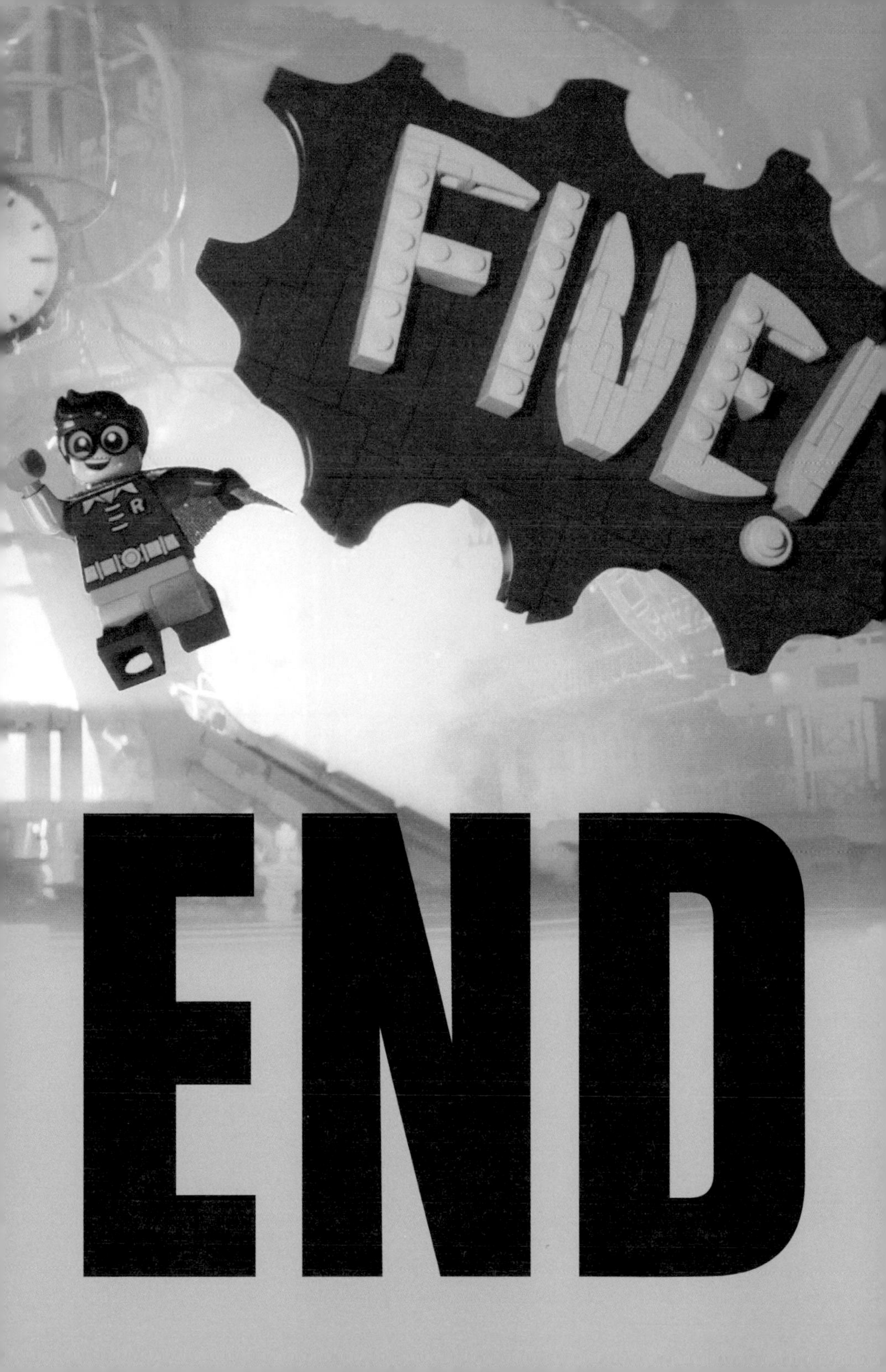
FINE!

END

BUILD YOUR THE LEGO® BATMAN MOVIE LIBRARY!

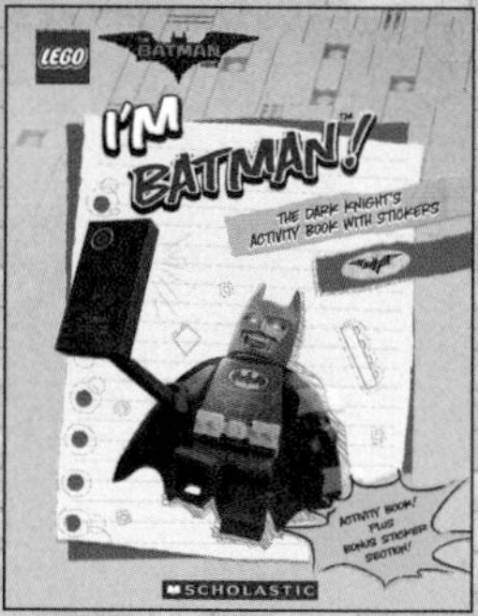
LEGO
I'M BATMAN!
THE DARK KNIGHT'S ACTIVITY BOOK WITH STICKERS
SCHOLASTIC

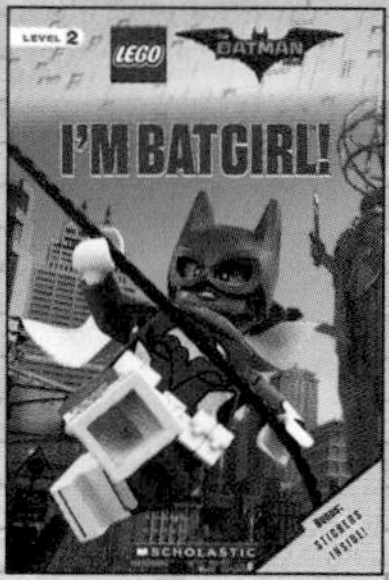
LEVEL 2
LEGO
BATMAN
I'M BATGIRL!
SCHOLASTIC

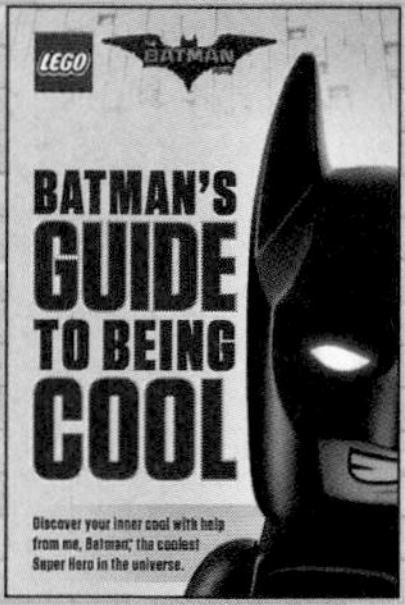
LEGO
BATMAN
BATMAN'S GUIDE TO BEING COOL
Discover your inner cool with help from me, Batman, the coolest Super Hero in the universe.

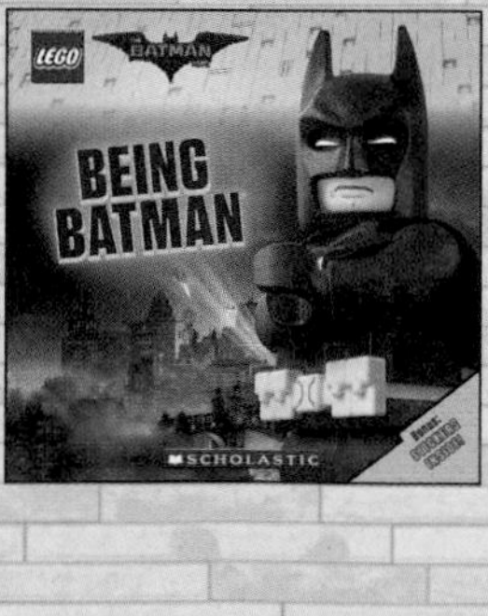
LEGO
BATMAN
BEING BATMAN
SCHOLASTIC

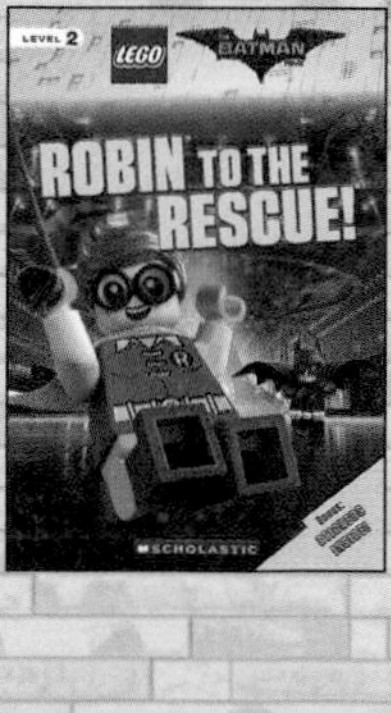
LEVEL 2
LEGO
BATMAN
ROBIN TO THE RESCUE!
SCHOLASTIC

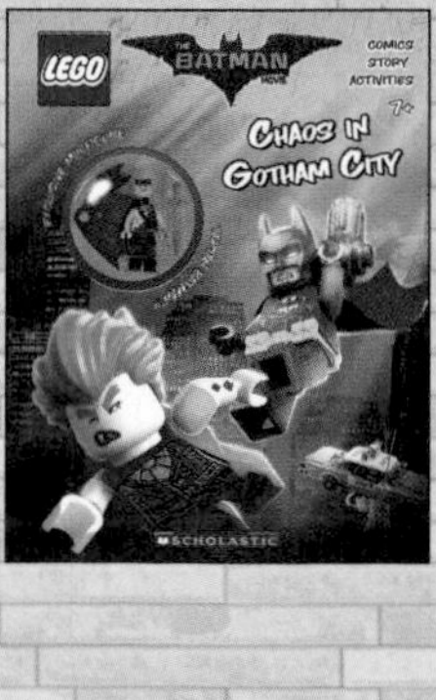
LEGO
BATMAN
COMICS
STORY
ACTIVITIES
7+
CHAOS IN GOTHAM CITY
SCHOLASTIC